Study Guide to Accompany

Professional
GARDE MANGER

A Comprehensive Guide
to Cold Food Preparation

Lou Sackett   Jaclyn Pestka   Wayne Gisslen, Consulting Author

WILEY
JOHN WILEY & SONS, INC.

Library of Congress Cataloging-in-Publication Data:

ISBN: 978-0-470-28473-5

Printed in the United States of America

V10014893_101719

CONTENTS

TO THE STUDENT

This ***Study Guide*** is the companion volume to ***Professional Garde Manger: A Comprehensive Guide to Cold Food Preparation.*** The ***Study Guide*** is designed to help you and your chef instructor evaluate your knowledge and understanding of the material presented in the ***Professional Garde Manger*** text.

Mastering the art and craft of garde manger is a many-faceted endeavor. You cannot learn garde manger solely by reading a book. In order to learn a particular garde manger topic you must proceed through several steps.

- **Read the chapter** of ***Professional Garde Manger*** that your instructor has assigned. As you read, it is recommended that you *take notes*. Use the section heads to create a chapter outline in your notebook, and under each outline head jot down a condensed version of the section information in your own words. Feel free to draw pictures and diagrams if you are a visual learner.

- **Complete the exercises** in the corresponding chapter of the ***Study Guide.*** The primary purpose of the ***Study Guide*** exercises is self-evaluation. Thus, it is counter-productive for you to simply copy from the text. For full benefit, *do the **Study Guide** exercises with the textbook closed.* If you do not know the answer to a particular question, first refer to your notes, and use the text as a last resort. If you find that you are constantly using your notes or the text, go back and re-read the chapter.

- **Participate in the lesson** your instructor has prepared. Listen carefully, and relate the information your instructor provides to the information you learned in reading the text. Add to the information already in your notebook by taking notes while your instructor lectures. Ask and answer questions when appropriate.

- **Practice** the chapter's methods and techniques in the classroom kitchen. If you have conscientiously worked on the first three steps, you will arrive in the kitchen armed with a sound foundation of knowledge. Your work will go faster and more smoothly, and you will be more likely to produce a successful product. After you have completed and presented your assigned product, pay close attention to your instructor's critique, and make sure you understand what, if anything, you should have done differently. Be attentive during the critique of other students' products, as well, and learn from their experiences.

- **Review** the chapter information in preparation for your instructor's learning assessment. Your completed ***Study Guide*** exercises are a valuable reviewing tool. If you can correctly and thoroughly answer the ***Study Guide*** questions without referring to the text or your notes, you are likely to do well on your instructor's assessment.

The chapters in the *Study Guide* correspond to the 18 chapters in *Professional Garde Manger*. All *Study Guide* chapters share the same basic structure. A brief *introduction* reviews the corresponding text chapter's content, and in some cases explains how the chapter content relates to that of other chapters. Following the introduction, a list of *chapter prerequisites* and *objectives* is reprinted from the text. These are not exercises but, rather, are provided to remind you of the specific skills and knowledge you should know before reading the chapter and work toward acquiring. The body of each *Study Guide* chapter consists of knowledge assessment sections. Each section contains exercise questions written in a particular format. Becoming familiar with the section types and their question formats will help you complete your *Study Guide* assignments quickly and correctly. Sections include:

Key Terms

This section appears in every *Study Guide* chapter. It tests your comprehension and retention of important terms presented throughout the chapter. Knowing and using the correct terms for tools, equipment, ingredients, techniques, and concepts are essential to effective communication in the garde manger kitchen and, additionally, demonstrate professionalism. To complete this exercise section, fill in the blank that precedes each definition with the correct term. Make sure to spell the term correctly. If, after self-evaluating this section, you find that you are having difficulty memorizing key terms, consider making flash cards.

Fill-in-the-Blank Questions

Sections consisting of fill-in-the-blank questions evaluate your knowledge of material found throughout the chapter. These questions are in sentence form, and involve basic recall of information. Read each sentence carefully, and write in the word or phrase that completes the sentence and makes it true.

Short-Answer Questions

Short-answer questions also cover material found throughout the chapter. They typically involve recall of information, frequently including memorization of processes. Some ask for explanations, and test your comprehension of certain concepts. In this format you are asked direct questions and provided with blank spaces in which you are to write your answers. Answer the questions as specifically and thoroughly as you can.

Multiple-Choice Questions

Multiple-choice questions evaluate recall and comprehension of material found throughout the chapter. This familiar question format consists of a stem, or incomplete sentence, and a selection of words that complete the sentence. One of these words makes the sentence completely true, and is the correct answer. The other words make the sentence false, or not completely true. Your task is to choose the correct answer and indicate it by circling or underlining it. When answering multiple-choice questions, pay particular attention to italicized words in the stems to ensure that you correctly understand the question. Some questions offer you the option of choosing two answer words. Be aware that the availability of a two-word option does not always make a two-word answer the correct choice.

Procedure Sections

For success in the classroom kitchen and in real-world food-service production you must know and understand basic garde manger procedures. When appropriate, your *Study Guide* chapters contain a section in which you are challenged to arrange the steps of important garde manger procedures in the proper order. While in the ***Professional Garde Manger*** text the procedures are explained in detail, in the *Study Guide* procedure sections the directions are condensed and some steps omitted or combined. To correctly order the procedures you must know the steps and work from memory.

Subject Sections

The evaluation tools in the *Study Guide* are designed to best represent the chapter's content. Thus, most *Study Guide* chapters additionally include specialized sections that focus on a particular subject covered in the corresponding text chapter. Examples include a "Know Your..." section in which you are asked to write the name of a classic sauce or well-known dish next to its description, and a "Troubleshooting" section in which you must deduce what caused a particular product flaw or failure. These sections frequently test your application and analysis skills, and are among the most challenging elements of the *Study Guide.* Each "Subject" section is formatted differently.

Short Essay Questions

Most *Study Guide* chapters conclude with a section of short essay questions. Many of these questions test your comprehension by asking you to summarize information from the text in your own words. Others require you to demonstrate practical application of information from the chapter, such as writing a menu or costing a buffet. Some involve drawing pictures or diagrams. Yet others elicit your opinion or challenge you to use your imagination. While many of these questions are open-ended and subjective, they nonetheless require effort and attention. Answer them thoughtfully and completely. Lined spaces have been provided for your written answers; your answer should be long enough to fill the spaces.

CHAPTER 1: THE GARDE MANGER PROFESSION

Chapter 1 involves the past, present, and future. The first part of the chapter discusses the history of the garde manger profession: how and why it was developed, and the artisan food producers and chefs who were instrumental in developing it. Knowing about early forms of food preservation helps you to understand many of today's garde manger products and procedures. Becoming familiar with the work of outstanding garde manger chefs enables you to reproduce classical garde manger dishes, and helps you develop your own, personal style of garde manger work. The chapter also introduces you to the specialized equipment you will use right now, in your study of garde manger. Finally, Chapter 1 helps you discover the many opportunities available in the field of modern garde manger. This information can help you plan your future career. Careful study of the material in this important opening chapter prepares you for success in completing the remaining chapters.

Before reading this chapter, you should have already learned
1. About basic food-service equipment.

After reading this chapter, you should be able to
1. Recount the history of the garde manger profession from early food preservation to modern times.
2. List the 12 attributes and characteristics of a successful garde manger chef.
3. List and define the 6 types of service.
4. Identify various types of food-service operations that provide opportunity for garde manger work.
5. Identify large and small equipment used for garde manger work.
6. Design a restaurant garde manger service line and set up a garde manger station.

A. Understanding the Term "Garde Manger"

Write a short definition for each.

1. garde manger (place) _____

2. garde manger (person) _____

3. garde manger (profession) _____

B. Key Terms

Fill in each blank with the correct term that is defined or described.

_____ 1. Serving large numbers of guests with a pre-planned menu of dishes.

_____ 2. A skilled food producer that makes high quality products primarily by hand using traditional methods.

_____ 3. Chef famous for classic garde manger presentations such as ice carvings, aspic and chaud-froid work, and other *pièces montées.*

_____ 4. The logical and fluid progression of movement; in *à la carte* service, refers to the assembly of dishes during turn-out.

_____ 5. A cuisine style combining classical French cooking with North American ingredients and taste preferences.

_____ 6. The chef credited with transitioning from Classical to Nouvelle Cuisine.

_____ 7. A drawing that lists and indicates the proper storage place of food components used in turn-out.

_____ 8. In European culinary history, the period of time from La Varenne through Escoffier.

_____ 9. High-quality, traditional-style, handmade food products.

_____ 10. Hybrid cuisine style that blends European cooking with Asian and Latin American ingredients.

_____ 11. Turn-out system in which the hot-line cook transfers hot food to the garde manger station for presentation as part of an otherwise cold dish.

_____ 12. Food service for large numbers of repeat customers, as in hospitals or schools.

_____ 13. The portion of a service line dedicated to turning out one particular type of preparation.

_____ 14. In creating the brigade system, he recognized garde manger as a separate, specialized field of culinary work.

_____ 15. Twentieth-century cooking style featuring lighter sauces, shorter cooking times, plate presentation.

_____ 16. Founder of modern French cuisine, he lightened and simplified European cooking.

_____ 17. A drawing that defines the boundaries of each station.

_____ 18. In food service, a row of large equipment units arranged for fast and efficient turn-out of food.

_____ 19. Service style in which foods are displayed on a table for guests to help themselves.

_____ 20. Place, person, or craft involving cold foods preparation.

C. Garde Manger Time Line

Match the time period with the garde manger event.

a. prehistoric times
b. the birth of agriculture (7000 B.C.E.) through the Dark Ages (1100 C.E.)
c. Middle Ages and Renaissance (1100 – 1600 C.E.)
d. mid 1600s
e. early 1800s
f. late 1800s to early 1900s
g. late 1800s through 1950s
h. 1960s through 1980s
i. 1980s through 2000
j. twenty-first century

1. _____ European estates and castles have underground food preservation and storage areas.

2. _____ Chefs blend European cooking techniques with Asian and Latin American ingredients to create Fusion Cuisine.

3. _____ La Varenne popularizes salads and makes garde manger work part of the kitchen.

4. _____ European chefs working in North America develop Continental cuisine and establish elaborate cold buffets in hotels.

5. _____ Humans learn to preserve foods by salting and drying them.

6. _____ Fernand Point trains young French chefs who go on to develop Nouvelle Cuisine.

7. _____ Carême creates elaborate pièces montées.

8. _____ Garde manger becomes even more important as salads are recognized as healthful food.

9. _____ Farm families improve food preservation methods and learn to make cheese.

10. _____ Escoffier institutes the kitchen brigade and recognizes garde manger as a separate specialty.

D. Service Types

Fill in each blank with the service type that is defined or described.

_____ 1. Pre-ordered plated foods are served to large numbers of guests at one time.

_____ 2. Customers order dishes individually from the menu, and dishes are prepared to order.

_____ 3. Individual orders of food are packed in disposable containers for pick-up or delivery.

_____ 4. Single-bite portions of finger foods are carried around the service area to guests standing or seated away from tables.

_____ 5. Platter presentations of food are placed on display for service to large numbers of guests.

_____ 6. Foods on covered plates are placed on trays or carts for delivery on premises.

E. Service Lines and Stations

1. Draw a line map for a single-line garde manger service line that must turn out the following menu items:

A. salads   B. cold appetizers and cold soups   C. cold sandwiches

Designate work stations for each type of menu item and label the large equipment you have chosen for each station.

2. The salad section of your garde manger service line must turn out the following salads:

a. tossed leaf lettuce salad with b. julienne carrots, c. sliced radishes, d. sliced cucumbers,
        e. grape tomatoes, f. ranch dressing
g. Caesar salad (with h. Caesar dressing)
i. shrimp salad on j. spring greens
k. chicken salad in l. tomato cup
m. spinach salad with n. bacon, o. mushrooms, and p. tomatoes in q. poppy seed dressing

Draw a station map showing storage locations of the components needed to turn out these salads.

E. Multiple-Choice Questions

1. The garde manger profession began in prehistory with:
   a. gathering culinary herbs
   b. hunting for meat animals
   c. preserving meat and fish with salt
   d. protecting domestic food animals from predators

2. This chef is credited with lightening and simplifying the overly elaborate food of the Middle Ages and early Renaissance:
   a. Carême
   b. La Varenne
   c. Escoffier
   d. Point

3. This cuisine style initiated the practice of chefs presenting food directly on the plate:
   a. Continental
   b. Medieval
   c. Nouvelle
   d. Fusion

4. By the end of the twentieth century, this long-established duty of the garde manger had become obsolete:
   a. cleaning salad greens
   b. curing meats and fish with salt
   c. preparing house-made mayonnaise
   d. fabricating cuts of meat and poultry

5. This cuisine style incorporated ingredients and techniques from around the world into European and North American garde manger work:
   a. Continental
   b. Medieval
   c. Nouvelle
   d. Fusion

6. This chef created the brigade system and physically separated garde manger from the hot line:
   a. Carême
   b. La Varenne
   c. Escoffier
   d. Point

7. This cuisine style combines classical French cooking with North American ingredients and taste preferences:
    a. Continental
    b. Medieval
    c. Nouvelle
    d. Fusion

8. This chef is known for creating fantastic *piéces montées*, the precursors of modern garde manger showpieces:
    a. Carême
    b. La Varenne
    c. Escoffier
    d. Point

9. In this service style, large numbers of seated guests are served the same menu of plated food.
    a. buffet
    b. banquet
    c. passed/butler
    d. á la carte

10. This garde manger career venue offers the largest variety of job opportunities:
    a. institutional
    b. private clubs
    c. hotel
    d. institutional

11. This term describes a portion of a service line dedicated to turning out one particular type of preparation:
    a. line map
    b. unit
    c. overshelf
    d. station

12. This document defines the boundaries of each station and indicates which menu items come out of each:
    a. line map
    b. flow chart
    c. prep list
    d. station map

F. Attributes and Characteristics Self-Check

Write a few sentences about how each attribute or characteristic of a successful garde manger chef applies to you. If you already possess an attribute or characteristic, give an example. If you do not yet possess an attribute or characteristic, write how you plan to acquire it.

1. Basic training and general experience: _____
_____
_____
_____

2. Formal culinary education: _____
_____
_____
_____

3. Manual dexterity: _____
_____
_____
_____

4. Physical stamina: _____
_____
_____
_____

5. Well-developed sense of taste: _____
_____
_____
_____

6. Artistic ability: _____
_____
_____
_____

7. Mathematical ability: _____
_____
_____
_____

8. Knowledge of food management and sanitation: _____

_____

_____

_____

9. Good interpersonal skills: _____

_____

_____

_____

10. Sense of urgency: _____

_____

_____

_____

11. Attention to detail: _____

_____

_____

_____

12. Ability to organize and plan: _____

_____

_____

_____

G. Careers in Garde Manger

Chapter 1 lists ten types of food service operations that offer career opportunities for the garde manger chef: restaurants, catering operations, hotels, cruise ships, institutions, private clubs, retail stores, artisan food production, product testing and development, and food styling. Choose one in which you are interested, and write a paragraph about it. Include a brief *summary of the work it entails*, and *why you would enjoy it.*

_____
_____
_____
_____
_____
_____
_____
_____
_____
_____
_____
_____

CHAPTER 2: SAUCES AND DRESSINGS

This chapter guides you through the preparation of sauces and dressings fundamental to garde manger work. The two most important, *vinaigrette* and *mayonnaise*, require not only skill and practice but also thorough understanding of the science of emulsions. Knowing how emulsions are created helps you avoid problems when preparing them and enables you to repair them when problems occur. Cold emulsion sauces, as well as dairy-based and fruit- and vegetable-based sauces, recur frequently throughout this text and throughout the garde manger repertoire. Thus, you should study this chapter carefully and work on these exercises until you have thoroughly mastered the material in it.

Before studying this chapter, you should have already learned
1. To prepare a meat or seafood *glace* (highly reduced stock).
2. To identify and use fresh and dried herbs.
3. To identify and use whole and ground spices.
4. To handle and prepare eggs and dairy products according to food safety guidelines.

After reading this chapter, you should be able to
1. Explain the chemistry of cold emulsions.
2. Prepare a successful vinaigrette by hand as well as in a mixer, blender, or food processor.
3. Repair a failed or broken vinaigrette.
4. Prepare mayonnaise by the traditional handmade procedure as well as in a mixer, blender, or food processor.
5. Repair both a failed and broken mayonnaise by several methods.
6. Prepare cold sauces based on dairy products.
7. Prepare cold sauces based on fruits and vegetables.
8. Use and store vinaigrettes, mayonnaise, and other cold sauces in accordance with food safety guidelines.

A. Key Terms

Fill in each blank with the correct term that is defined or described.

_____ 1. A fluid accompaniment to solid food.

_____ 2. A sauce used to enhance salads and sandwiches, and as a dip.

_____ 3. A term to describe the acrid odor and bad flavor of spoiled oil.

_____ 4. The role that oil plays in the emulsion of a standard vinaigrette.

_____ 5. The emulsifier found in egg yolk.

_____ 6. A basic mayonnaise having no particularly assertive flavors.

_____ 7. A uniform mixture of two normally unmixable substances.

_____ 8. An emulsion sauce that will eventually separate, even when properly handled and stored.

_____ 9. An emulsion sauce that remains in emulsion when properly handled and stored.

_____ 10. An oil made completely from olives, extracted by purely physical processes that do not include heat or chemicals.

_____ 11. A tart, unfermented condiment made from unripe wine grapes.

_____ 12. A coarse textured, rustic sauce made from tomatoes or other soft, juicy vegetables or fruits.

_____ 13. Resting a sauce or other preparation so that the flavors have time to develop.

_____ 14. A microscopic organism introduced into wine that causes an additional acetous fermentation and changes it into vinegar.

_____ 15. Term used to describe visible bands that form on the surface of a thick substance, such as mayonnaise, when it falls back into a bowl.

_____ 16. Term to describe mayonnaise that is over-thickened and oily.

_____ 17. Term used to describe the texture of a sauce thick enough to coat a cool, clean, metal spoon yet thin enough to flow on the plate.

_____ 18. A puréed sauce made from a vegetable or fruit.

_____ 19. The emulsifier found in dairy products.

_____ 20. Occurs when water molecules cling tightly to each other and form a kind of elastic sheet.

B. Fill-in-the-Blank Questions

Fill in the blank to correctly complete the statement.

1. Mayonnaise is an example of a _____ emulsion.

2. The three essential ingredients in vinaigrette are _____, _____, and _____.

3. The three major enemies of oil are _____, _____, and _____.

4. When a _____ is added to an emulsion, it prevents separation by preventing dispersed droplets from combining.

5. The _____ component is typically considered to be the primary flavor of a vinaigrette.

6. A _____ is a cold sauce having a pronounced acidic flavor.

7. The addition of egg yolk creates a stable vinaigrette because it contains the emulsifier _____.

8. In the composition of a standard vinaigrette, the vinegar is the _____ phase and the oil is the _____ phase.

9. Water molecules cling together because they are highly _____.

10. Refrigerated mayonnaise should be brought to _____ temperature before stirring or whipping.

C. Procedures

Correctly number the steps in the following procedures.

Note: The directions have been condensed and some steps omitted or combined. You must think about the procedures and demonstrate your understanding; do not expect to copy from the text.

1. Basic procedure for making vinaigrette:

_____ Combine the vinegar and seasonings in the bowl.

_____ Taste and correct the flavor balance.

_____ Have all ingredients at room temperature.

_____ Whip until frothy.

_____ Whip in the oil in a thin stream.

13

2. Procedure for making mayonnaise (traditional method):

_____ Whip the yolks, vinegar or lemon juice, and salt in a bowl until light and frothy.

_____ Whip in oil, one drop at a time, until the emulsion begins to catch.

_____ Have ready boiling water and all ingredients at room temperature.

_____ Stir in a few drops of boiling water.

_____ Refrigerate 1 to 2 hours.

_____ Taste and correct the seasoning.

_____ Slow the speed of whipping to stirring, and increase the rate at which you add the oil (thin the consistency as necessary).

3. Procedure for making fruit coulis:

_____ Skin and trim the fruit, discarding cores, hull, seeds, and unripe areas.

_____ Chop the fruit into small pieces.

_____ Strain the fruit purée.

_____ Blanch and refresh the fruit to loosen its skin.

_____ Purée the fruit in a blender or food processor.

4. Procedure for making fresh tomato salsa:

_____ Add the tomatoes to the aromatics and grind to a rough purée.

_____ Balance flavor with acidic ingredient, if needed.

_____ Mash the aromatics into a rough paste.

_____ Place chopped aromatic vegetables in a mortar.

_____ Stir in herbs.

D. Know Your Sauces and Dressings

Correctly name each sauce or dressing described below.

1. _____ mayonnaise with heavy cream, mustard, lemon juice

2. _____ Dijon mustard, sour pickles, capers, parsley, tarragon, chervil, and anchovy paste

3. _____ mayonnaise with cooked and puréed spinach watercress, parsley, chervil, and tarragon

4. _____ tomatillos, Serrano chiles, garlic, and cilantro

5. _____ mayonnaise with ketchup, sweet relish, horseradish, and pimiento

6. _____ mayonnaise with crumbled blue cheese and heavy cream

7. _____ mayonnaise with puréed spinach, watercress, parsley, and tarragon

8. _____ Mediterranean mayonnaise with minced garlic, minced lemon zest

9. _____ egg, anchovies, grated Reggiano Parmesan cheese, olive oil

10. _____ mayonnaise with prepared horseradish and heavy cream

E. Multiple-Choice Questions

1. Which is *not* an essential component in a vinaigrette?
   a. salad oil
   b. salt
   c. sugar
   d. vinegar

2. *Verjus* is made from:
   a. grapes
   b. apples
   c. grain
   d. citrus fruits

3. Vinegar contains:
   a. lactic acid
   b. malic acid
   c. carbolic acid
   d. acetic acid

4. Which is/are characteristic of extra-virgin olive oil?
    a. made completely from olives
    b. made by physical processes
    c. no heat applied
    d. (a. and c.)
    e. (a., b., and c.)

5. In an emulsion, the liquid that is broken up into tiny droplets is called the:
    a. continuous phase
    b. static phase
    c. suspended phase
    d. dispersed phase

6. In an emulsion, the liquid surrounding the tiny droplets is called the:
    a. continuous phase
    b. static phase
    c. suspended phase
    d. dispersed phase

7. Molecules that have a slight positive charge on one side and slight negative charge on the other side are called:
    a. polar
    b. surface tense
    c. stable
    d. hydrostatic

8. A vinaigrette made with minced shallot, minced garlic, and minced fresh thyme should be re-tasted after a mellowing period of:
    a. 5 minutes
    b. 1/2 hour
    c. 1 hour
    d. 2 hours

9. Which is an emulsifier found in egg yolks?
    a. casein
    b. triglyceride
    c. fatty acid
    d. lecithin

10. Mayonnaise is often finished with a little:
    a. egg yolk
    b. butter
    c. boiling water
    d. ice water

F. Troubleshooting Sauces and Dressings

1. A mayonnaise that you made turned green/gray. What went wrong?

_____

_____

_____

_____

How can it be fixed? _____

_____

_____

2. A vinaigrette that you made will not stay in a temporary emulsion.
What went wrong? _____

_____

_____

_____

_____

How can it be fixed? _____

_____

_____

3. A mayonnaise that you made has a thick and greasy mouthfeel.
What went wrong? _____

_____

_____

_____

How can it be fixed? _____

_____

_____

4. A neutral mayonnaise that you made was successful until you added additional ingredients.
What went wrong? _____

_____

_____

How can it be fixed? _____

_____

_____

5. The double batch of mayonnaise that you made is thin and will not thicken.
What went wrong? _____

_____

_____

_____

How can it be fixed? _____

_____

_____

G. Short Essay Question

1. Explain in your own words the science of emulsions. In sauce making, what are the two substances that are emulsified together? On a molecular level, how does this happen? On a separate piece of paper, draw pictures to illustrate your explanation.

_____

_____

_____

_____

_____

_____

_____

_____

_____

_____

_____

_____

_____

_____

_____

_____

CHAPTER 3: SIMPLE SALADS AND TOSSED SALADS

Although simple salads are fast and easy to prepare, serving consistently excellent salads requires informed purchasing, correct storage, and proper preparation. Blending salad greens into interesting combinations with complementary dressings requires knowledge and a discerning palate. The questions in this section are designed to test your salad smarts.

Before studying this chapter, you should already
1. Have read "How to Use This Book," pages xxviii–xxxiii, and understand the professional recipe format.
2. Know basic sanitation procedures for products served raw.
3. Know state and local regulations for food-service glove use.

After reading this chapter, you should be able to
1. Explain the differences between simple salads and tossed salads.
2. List the five salad greens flavor groups and identify the various greens that belong to each group.
3. Discuss the advantages and disadvantages of the various market forms in which salad greens are available.
4. Recognize signs of quality in salad greens.
5. Properly store, clean, and fabricate salad greens.
6. Prepare salads using à la carte, tableside, family-style, and banquet procedures.
7. Create salads that are attractive, well balanced, and seasonal.

A. Key Terms

Fill in each blank with the correct term that is defined or described.

_____ 1. A combination of leafy greens tossed with a vinaigrette dressing and having minimal garnishes.

_____ 2. A green salad mixed or topped with a variety of brightly colored vegetable garnishes.

_____ 3. Whole, tiny herb leaves.

_____ 4. The term used for describing greens whose cells are full of water; evidenced by leaves that stand upright when the bunch is picked up.

_____ 5. Describes a lettuce or other green that is over-mature, having grown thick, tall stalks and flattened leaves.

19

_____ 6. Brown discoloration on lettuce or other salad greens.

_____ 7. The first shoots produced by plant seeds, harvested before the true leaves have formed.

_____ 8. Tiny, lacy-textured greens consisting of only the stem and first true leaves.

_____ 9. The young immature leaves of standard lettuces and other salad greens.

_____ 10. Brand name mixtures of various greens.

_____ 11. The name given to a mixture of baby lettuces, young arugula, and immature red chicory that originated in Provence, France.

_____ 12. A popular blend of greens that can contains virtually any baby green or specialty green.

_____ 13. The practice of growing plants in water-based nutrient solutions.

_____ 14. Greens packaged with their root ball submerged in a shallow well of water.

_____ 15. Pansy petals, delicate miniature orchids, and peppery nasturtium blossoms are examples of these.

B. Fill-in-the-Blank Questions

Fill in the blank to correctly complete the statement.

1. Most salad greens should be stored between _____ and _____ degrees F (or C).

2. Two methods commonly used for fabricating salad greens are _____ and _____.

3. Salad plates should be kept at a _____ temperature.

4. Salad greens may be dried in a _____ or in a _____.

5. Commercially grown greens should be stored in _____ as long as possible.

6. In fine-dining restaurants, salads are prepared _____.

7. For banquets, salads are usually prepared _____.

8. Sturdy greens may be tossed with a _____ dressing, while delicate greens are best with a _____ dressing.

9. In formal European dining, simple salads are served _____.

10. Fresh, high-quality salad greens appear _____.

C. Short-Answer Questions

1. List three examples of the following salad greens flavor groups.

a. Lettuces:

1. _____ 2. _____ 3. _____

b. Spinach and beet greens:

1. _____ 2. _____ 3. _____

c. Mild-flavored brassicas:

1. _____ 2. _____ 3. _____

d. Spicy brassicas:

1. _____ 2. _____ 3. _____

e. Bitter greens:

1. _____ 2. _____ 3. _____

2. Explain the difference between a simple salad and a complex salad.

_____

_____

_____.

3. The four steps in cleaning salad greens are:

step #1 _____ step #3 _____

step #2 _____ step #4 _____

4. When properly dressing a salad, your goal is to _____

_____.

5. Two negative results of improperly dried salad greens are:

a. _____

b. _____

D. Multiple-Choice Questions

1. To qualify as a simple salad, a salad may *not* include:
    a. toasted walnuts
    b. edible flowers
    c. Russian dressing
    d. vinaigrette dressing

2. Which belongs to the spicy brassicas flavor group?
    a. tatsoi
    b. arugula
    c. lolla rossa
    d. escarole

3. Which is not an immature salad green?
    a. living lettuce
    b. sprouts
    c. micro-greens
    d. baby greens

4. Greens that are grown without soil are called:
    a. hygroscopic
    b. hydrophilic
    c. hydrophobic
    d. hydroponic

5. Which is a characteristic of pre-cleaned, pre-fabricated greens?
    a. low labor
    b. low cost
    c. always safe
    d. long keeping

6. Salad greens that are overgrown and bitter are called:
    a. rusty
    b. turgid
    c. wilted
    d. bolted

7. Slightly wilted greens can be refreshed by soaking them in cold water for:
    a. 5 minutes
    b. 20 minutes
    c. 1 hour
    d. 2 hours

8. In North America, tableside salad preparation is most frequently associated with:
    a. Cobb salad
    b. Salade Niçoise
    c. taco salad
    d. Caesar salad

9. In fine dining restaurants, dressings for à la carte service salads are:
    a. mixed with the greens to order by the garde manger chef
    b. mixed with the greens ahead of time by the garde manger chef
    c. presented on the side by the server
    d. mixed with the salad by the server

10. In casual and family restaurants, dressings for à la carte service salads are:
    a. mixed with the greens to order by the garde manger chef
    b. mixed with the greens ahead of time by the gar
    c. presented on the side by the server
    d. mixed with the salad by the server

E. Short Essay Questions

1. Discuss seasonality in salad making. Include in your discussion an example of a summer season salad and a winter season salad.

_____

_____

_____

_____

_____

_____

_____

2. Outline your strategy for serving only the freshest salads in your operation. Include the topics of purchasing, storage, and preparation in your plan.

_____

_____

_____

_____

_____

_____

_____

CHAPTER 4: COLD VEGETABLES AND FRUITS

The goal of this chapter is to build upon the knowledge you have already gained in your introductory cooking classes and refine your understanding of vegetable and fruit preparation. It focuses on techniques specific to cold presentations, both raw and cooked, and gives detailed instructions for purchasing, storing, and fabricating vegetables and fruits intended for cold service. Mastering the information in this chapter is essential for success in preparing the vegetable- and fruit-based complex salads, soups, hors d'oeuvres, and garnishes and decorations covered in subsequent chapters. Check your knowledge of vegetable and fruit preparation by correctly answering the questions in this workbook chapter.

Before studying this chapter, you should already
1. Have read "How to Use This Book," pages xxviii–xxxiii, and understand the professional recipe format.
2. Be able to identify standard vegetables and fruits, and to evaluate them for quality.
3. Know how to properly store standard vegetables and fruits in order to retain quality.
4. Be able to fabricate standard vegetables and fruits, including the use of classic cuts.
5. Be able to prevent enzymatic browning of vegetables and fruits using various techniques.

After reading this chapter, you should be able to
1. Preserve texture, color, flavor, and nutrients when cooking vegetables and fruits for cold service.
2. List the six changes that occur during the fruit ripening process.
3. Identify specialty vegetables and fruits, and fabricate them for various garde manger preparations.
4. Prepare vegetables to be served cold by the steaming, blanching, poaching, stewing, braising, roasting, and grilling methods.
5. Cook vegetables to the appropriate degree of doneness for various garde manger applications.
6. Manage the ripening of fruits through proper purchasing and storage.
7. Create attractive fruit platters.

A. Key Terms
Fill in each blank with the correct term that is defined or described.

_____ 1. Vegetables cooked to a texture that is tender but with just a little resistance to the bite.

_____ 2. The process by which a mature fruit completes its life cycle.

_____ 3. The term used to describe the removal of spoiled or damaged fruit from other fruits.

_____ 4. The part of a vegetable or fruit that was cut during harvesting.

_____ 5. Applied by some commercial growers to combat moisture loss in many fruits and vegetables after harvesting.

_____ 6. Seeds from vegetables and fruits that have been handed down from past generations.

_____ 7. Fruits and vegetables that are grown without the use of chemical fertilizers, pesticides, and herbicides.

_____ 8. The reproductive organ, specifically the ovary, of a seed plant.

_____ 9. The procedure used to replace lost moisture and firm the texture of vegetables by immersing them in ice water after they have been peeled and fabricated.

_____ 10. The gas produced by ripening fruit.

_____ 11. The classic French raw vegetable dish.

_____ 12. The natural progression of ripening eventually leads to this.

_____ 13. A dish consisting of whole, intact cold vegetables, or a single type of cold vegetable.

_____ 14. The name of the peeling technique used to remove very tough skin from vegetables.

_____ 15. Literally "to the tooth," cooked enough to lose raw taste but retain crisp texture.

_____ 16. The term to describe vegetables and fruits cooked to complete tenderness.

_____ 17. Responsible for the color of fruits and vegetables.

_____ 18. The primary cell structure found in vegetables.

_____ 19. The technique to quickly and efficiently stop the process of carryover cooking in steamed and blanched foods.

_____ 20. The term for properly blanching several types of vegetables in the same water.

_____ 21. After immersing vegetables in boiling water, the time it takes to compensate for the drop in temperature and to regain the boil.

_____ 22. Boiling a food for a short period of time in order to partially cook it, or to fully cook it to a firm texture.

_____ 23. Cooking food completely submerged in a flavorful liquid at a low temperature.

_____ 24. The French culinary term for a flavorful poaching liquid.

_____ 25. A specialized poaching liquid frequently used for artichokes.

B. Fill-in-the-Blank Questions

Fill in the blank to correctly complete the statement.

1. Cauliflower and broccoli are members of the _____ vegetable family.

2. Carrots and beets are members of the _____ vegetable family.

3. Tomatoes and eggplants are members of the _____ vegetable family.

4. Cucumbers and zucchini are members of the _____ vegetable family.

5. Onions and shallots are members of the _____ vegetable family.

6. Green beans and lima beans are members of the _____ vegetable family.

7. Vegetable colors are created by the presence of plant _____.

8. The pigment present in green vegetables is _____.

9. The pigment present in orange vegetables is _____.

10. Vegetable and fruit cultivars grown from seeds handed down from past generations are known as _____.

11. _____ is the process by which a mature fruit completes its life cycle.

12. As a fruit ripens, the sugar content _____.

13. As a fruit ripens, the acid content _____.

14. As a fruit ripens, the aroma _____.

15. As a fruit ripens, the flavor _____.

16. One of the most important factors in ripening is the action of a simple hydrocarbon gas called _____.

17. Some cut fruits and vegetables discolor due to _____.

18. Cut fruits and vegetables that may discolor should be brushed with _____ or soaked in _____.

19. Peeled, raw potatoes should be stored in _____.

20. Vegetables for crudités can be held for a short time in _____ to crisp them.

21. To prevent ripe fruit from becoming over-ripe or decaying, store _____.

22. Store un-cut potatoes, onions, garlic, and shallots _____.

23. For best flavor and texture, tomatoes should be stored _____.

24. Store under-ripe fruit in an open container between _____ and _____ degrees F.

25. To speed the process of ripening under-ripe fruit, place a _____ with the fruit in a closed container.

C. Multiple-Choice Questions

1. Which characteristic does not contribute to a vegetable's texture?
    a. cellulose content
    b. freshness
    c. sugar content
    d. maturity

2. Acidic ingredients destroy:
    a. carotene
    b. chlorophyll
    c. anthocyanins
    d. anthoxanthins

3. Which is *not* a requirement of certified organic produce?
   a. must be grown without the use of chemical fertilizers, pesticides, and herbicides
   b. must not be subjected to biotechnology or irradiation
   c. must confirm to USDA nutritional requirements
   d. must not be fertilized with reprocessed sewage

4. To prevent discoloration, fruits subject to enzymatic browning can be treated with:
   a. an approved food sanitizing solution
   b. an ascorbic acid solution
   c. a sodium nitrite solution
   d. acidulated water
   e. (b. and d.)
   f. (c. and d.)

5. To speed ripening, store fruits:
   a. enclosed, room temperature, with a cut apple
   b. open, refrigerated, with a cut apple
   c. enclosed, on a stovetop, with a cut lemon
   d. open, room temperature, sprayed with water at intervals

6. One way to halt or slow deterioration in fresh vegetables is to:
   a. submerge in a tub of water and refrigerate
   b. wrap tight in plastic film and refrigerate
   c. seal in a plastic bag with a cut apple and refrigerate
   d. blanch and refresh, drain, place in container, and refrigerate

7. When cleaning strawberries, soak them in water for:
   a. less than 1 minute
   b. 10 minutes
   c. 1/2 hour
   d. 2 hours

8. Which is *not* a benefit of peeling vegetables?
   a. better mouthfeel
   b. even cooking
   c. better nutrition
   d. wax removal

9. Fabricated vegetables for raw service should be crisped in ice water for:
   a. less than 1 minute
   b. 10 minutes
   c. 1/2 hour
   d. 2 hours

10. The correct texture of green beans intended for salads is:
    a. raw
    b. al dente
    c. *à point*
    d. fork-tender
    e. (a. and b.)
    f. (b. and c.)

11. You normally cook vegetables for salads in a stove-top steamer, but a pressure steamer has just been installed in your kitchen. When using it, your cooking time should be:
    a. longer
    b. shorter
    c. the same

12. Which vegetable can be successfully cooked by poaching?
    a. green beans
    b. carrots
    c. broccoli
    d. (a. and b.)
    e. (b. and c.)

D. Purchasing Vegetables and Fruits

1. In order for the USDA to recognize a vegetable or fruit as certified organic produce, it must meet the following four criteria:

1. _____

2. _____

3. _____

4. _____

2. List the five quality characteristics used when evaluating vegetables and fruits for purchase. For each characteristic, give an example citing a particular fruit.

1._____

_____

_____

2._____

_____

_____

3._____

_____

_____

4._____

_____

_____

5._____

_____

_____

3. List the three characteristics that help determine whether a fruit is ripe. For each characteristic, give an example citing a particular fruit.

1._____

(example)

_____

_____

2._____

(example)

_____

_____

3._____

(example)

_____

_____

E. Vegetable and Fruit Fabrication and Cooking

1. List the four basic steps in vegetable and fruit fabrication and summarize the important points for each.

step #1 _____

_____

_____

step #2 _____

_____

_____

step #3 _____

_____

_____

step #4 _____

_____

_____

2. List and define the three basic levels of doneness for vegetables and fruits.

1. _____

_____

2. _____

_____

3. _____

_____

3. List and describe the six steps in blanching and refreshing.

step #1 _____

_____

step #2 _____

_____

step #3 _____

_____

step #4 _____

_____

step #5 _____

_____

step #6 _____

_____

4. Explain the fabrication method for the following vegetable preparations. Draw pictures to illustrate your explanations.

a. roasted peppers

b. artichoke hearts

c. asparagus

d. artichoke bottoms

e. whole leeks

CHAPTER 5: COMPLEX SALADS

This chapter guides you in combining the sauces and dressings presented in Chapter 2 with the cold vegetable and fruit preparations covered in Chapter 4 to make a variety of complex salads. Complex salads that include leafy greens require understanding of Chapter 3 information, as well. Make sure that you have mastered the methods and techniques introduced in Chapters 2, 3, and 4 before proceeding to this one.

While many of the complex salad recipes in this chapter are straightforward and easy to present, some of the more advanced arranged salad presentations require significant technical skill. Success in presenting these dishes cannot be learned from a book, but rather requires repeated practice in plating them. However, arriving in the classroom kitchen with a solid understanding of the six presentation styles saves time and gives you a clear advantage.

Test your knowledge of complex salad preparation and presentation by correctly answering all of the questions in this workbook chapter.

Before studying this chapter, you should already
1. Have read "How to Use This Book," pp. xxviii–xxxiii, and understand the professional recipe format.
2. Know how to perform basic meat, poultry, and seafood preparation and cooking methods.

After reading this chapter, you should be able to
1. Explain the difference between simple salads and complex salads
2. Prepare each type of complex salad presented in this chapter in accordance with food safety practices.
3. Plate arranged salads in the bedded, mounded, flat, molded, and stacked presentation styles.
4. Use specialized garde manger tools to prepare contemporary arranged salads.
5. Create your own signature complex salads following the guidelines given in the chapter.

A. Key Terms
Fill in each blank with the term that is defined or described.

_____ 1. Salads made up of raw or cooked vegetables or fruits, starches or legumes, or protein foods.

_____ 2. In this presentation style, all of the salad ingredients are combined together with the dressing and mounded on a plate or platter.

_____ 3. In this presentation style, each of the various elements of the salad is dressed or seasoned separately and then all are assembled together on the plate.

_____ 4. Salads consisting of vegetables, legumes, grains, or starches that are typically served as accompaniments.

_____ 5. Salads that are composed primarily of diced meat, poultry, or seafood mixed with a thick dressing and are traditionally served center of plate.

_____ 6. Salads consisting of an equal mixture of vegetables, starches, and proteins, hence containing the three elements of a complete entrée.

_____ 7. Vegetables that exude moisture when mixed with dressings and allowed to stand for a period of time are said to do this.

_____ 8. Any salad having a thick dressing that holds the ingredients together in a cohesive mass is referred to as this type of salad.

_____ 9. An attractive piece of lettuce placed on a plate under a complex salad.

_____ 10. A technique in which sauces and dressings are used to create artistic designs on the plate.

_____ 11. The raised outer rim of a plate that serves as the "frame" for the plated food composition.

_____ 12. The main part of the plate inside the rim.

_____ 13. A directive that indicates a specific place on the perimeter of a plate.

_____ 14. A simple salad used as a component of a complex salad, usually placed on the plate under the other elements of the presentation.

_____ 15. In food presentation, a molded base of various shapes.

_____ 16. A square or rectangular block of food that serves as a base.

B. Fill-in-the-Blank Questions

Fill in the blank to correctly complete the statement.

1. To preserve the bright green color of vegetables in a complex salad _____

_____.

2. Raw onions should be added to complex salads _____.

3. The four types of complex side salads are: _____, _____,

_____, and _____.

4. Three techniques that can be used to avoid "watering out" of high-moisture complex salad

ingredients are: _____, _____,

and _____.

5. Complex salads may include three basic types of legumes: _____,

_____, and _____.

6. To be perceived as a good value, bound protein salads should contain a relatively low

proportion of _____.

7. Complete salads consist of all three elements of a nutritionally balanced meal: a

_____, a _____, and a _____.

8. When preparing fruit salads, two types of ingredients you should hold out and add at the last

before service are _____ and _____.

9. At the simplest level, an arranged salad has these three elements: _____,

_____, and _____.

C. Know Your Classic Complex Salads

Name the following well-known complex salads.

_____ 1. Mayonnaise-bound salad containing diced potatoes,
beets, carrots, and peas.

_____ 2. Middle Eastern salad comprised of bulgur wheat,
tomatoes, and parsley that is dressed with olive oil and
lemon juice.

_____ 3. Mixture of cool cooked seafood in a lemon vinaigrette.

_____ 4. Mayonnaise-bound salad of apples, celery, and walnuts.

_____ 5. Cone-shaped mound of lettuce and watercress topped with stripes of crumbled bacon, blue cheese, hard-cooked egg, diced tomatoes, and diced chicken.

_____ 6. Crab salad bound with a sweet pink mayonnaise dressing, typically served in an avocado half with tomato, hard-cooked egg, and black olives.

_____ 7. Arranged salad of tuna vinaigrette, French potato salad, green beans vinaigrette, and Mediterranean garnishes.

_____ 8. Sliced tomatoes and mozzarella cheese with garlic, olive oil, and fresh basil.

D. Short-Answer Questions

1. Explain the difference between a simple salad and a complex salad.

simple: _____

complex: _____

2. List five guidelines for complex salads food safety.

a. _____

b. _____

c. _____

d. _____

e. _____

3. Explain "mellowing time" as it refers to complex salads, and give an example.

_____

_____

example: _____

4. List and describe the two methods of cooking potatoes for potato salad.

method: _____

description: _____

_____

method: _____

description: _____

_____

5. List six guidelines for preparing arranged salads.

a. _____

b. _____

c. _____

d. _____

e. _____

f. _____

E. Multiple-Choice Questions

1. Which of the following is not an example of a complex salad?
   a. potato salad
   b. Cobb salad
   c. Caesar salad
   d. shrimp salad

2. A bound protein salads is typically served as a:
   a. side dish   d. sandwich filling
   b. appetizer   e. (a. and b.)
   c. main dish   f. (c. and d.)

3. In modern menu planning, a complex side salad should *not* accompany:
    a. a cold main dish
    b. a grilled main dish
    c. a deep-fried main dish
    d. a braised main dish

4. Which technique is not recommended to prevent raw vegetables from watering out?
    a. acidulating
    b. salting
    c. scalding
    d. pre-dressing

5. Allowing mellowing time, followed by tasting and evaluation, ensures that a complex salad will have the proper:
    a. mouthfeel
    b. color
    c. seasoning
    d. (a. and c.)
    e. (a. and b.)

6. If russet potatoes are to be used for potato salad, they should be:
    a. baked, cooled, and scooped from their skins
    b. boiled, cooled, peeled, and diced
    c. peeled, diced, poached, and cooled
    d. any of the above methods

7. Pasta for pasta salads should be:
    a. boiled, drained, refreshed, and dressed at room temperature
    b. boiled, drained, open-pan cooled, and dressed while warm
    c. boiled, drained, refreshed, refrigerated, and dressed when cold
    d. any of the above methods

8. The main ingredient of a bound protein salad intended as a sandwich filling should be fabricated into:
    a. 1-inch (2.5 cm) dice
    b. 1/2-inch (1.25 cm) dice
    c. coarse chop
    d. brunoise cuts

9. In correct plate presentation, food should never be placed on/in the:
   a. front of plate
   b. 4 o'clock position
   c. plate well
   d. plate rim

10. The classic Salade Niçoise is an example of which presentation type?
   a. bedded
   b. mounded
   c. flat
   d. stacked

11. The primary advantage of the stacked salad presentation style is:
   a. appearance
   b. low labor cost
   c. low food cost
   d. speed of turn-out

12. Molded salads often function as a _____ for other salad elements.
   a. liner
   b. socle
   c. bed
   d. topping

F. Understanding Arranged Salad Presentations

Demonstrate your understanding of arranged salads by describing and illustrating each of the five presentation styles.

a. Bedded Salads
Write a description: Draw a picture:

_____
_____
_____
_____

b. Mounded Salads
Write a description: Draw a picture:

_____
_____
_____
_____

c. Flat Salads
Write a description: Draw a picture:

_____
_____
_____
_____

d. Molded Salads
Write a description: Draw a picture:

_____
_____
_____
_____

e. Stacked Salads
Write a description: Draw a picture:

_____
_____
_____
_____

CHAPTER 6: COLD SEAFOOD

In many ways the preparation of seafood for cold service is similar to that of hot seafood. However, many garde manger seafood dishes require specialized knowledge and advanced techniques beyond the scope of standard seafood cookery. Mastering the information in this chapter will help you achieve success in preparing cold seafood.

Before studying this chapter, you should already
1. Have read "How to Use This Book," pages xxviii–xxxiii, and understand the professional recipe format.
2. Know basic information about seafood and have mastered basic fabrication and cooking methods for it.
3. Have basic familiarity with unflavored commercial gelatin and the techniques used in working with it.

After reading this chapter, you should be able to
1. Identify categories of seafood, and select fish and shellfish appropriate for use in cold service.
2. Poach, steam, pan-steam, shallow-poach, and grill fish and shellfish for use in cold service.
3. Prepare fish and shellfish by "cooking" them with acidic ingredients.
4. Prepare seafood mousses and use to create terrines, timbales, and other formed presentations.
5. Serve raw fish and shellfish in accordance with food safety guidelines.
6. Identify, purchase, and correctly serve caviar.

A. Key Terms

Fill in the blank with the term that is defined or described.

_____ 1. A non-mammal animal food derived from both fresh and saltwater sources.

_____ 2. The liquid inside an oyster shell.

_____ 3. Aquatic animal having a complex segmented exterior shell and legs.

_____ 4. An aquatic animal having a bony interior skeleton and fin.

_____ 5. An aquatic animal similar to a bivalve, but having only one exterior shell section.

_____ 6. A mollusk having tentacles and a defined head.

_____ 7. Chilled seafood tossed or topped with a sauce, typically served in a stemmed glass.

_____ 8. A flavorful liquid made by simmering together mirepoix, a bouquet garni, white wine, and water.

_____ 9. Used to describe a dish in which the *cuisson* is served as a broth or very light sauce along with the seafood.

_____ 10. Cooking food in an enclosed space completely surrounded by the vapor produced by water heated to temperatures above 212°F (100°C).

_____ 11. Consists of a full-flavored base of cooked, puréed food lightened with whipped cream and/or beaten egg whites, and served with no further cooking.

_____ 12. Translates as "little salt" in Russian.

_____ 13. A technique used to incorporate a light, airy substance into a heavier one.

_____ 14. A sauce based on tomato ketchup and prepared horseradish.

_____ 15. The practice of raising seafood in a controlled environment.

_____ 16. Italian for "raw fish."

_____ 17. The preserved roe, or eggs, of fish.

_____ 18. Term used to describe individual fish eggs.

_____ 19. A small, thin buckwheat pancake.

_____ 20. A sauce made from white wine, vinegar, and cracked peppercorns.

_____ 21. The Italian name for salted, pressed tuna roe.

_____ 22. The Greek name for various salted and pressed fish roes.

_____ 23. Japanese green horseradish.

_____ 24. Asian white radish.

_____ 25. An Asian dish consisting of raw fish and other types of seafood, served simply, and with few embellishments.

_____ 26. An Asian dish comprised of cooked, cooled rice seasoned with vinegar, sugar, and salt, frequently topped with raw or cooked seafood.

_____ 27. The hairy filament found in a mussel.

_____ 28. Giant clam.

_____ 29. To remove sand from clams or other bivalves by soaking them in brine.

_____ 30. A freshly shucked oyster served in a chilled shot glass topped with hot sauce and vodka.

B. Shellfish Purchasing

1. Name the three most common market sizes for Eastern hard shell clams.

1._____   2._____   3._____

2. Shrimp are classified by count per pound or per half-kilo. Complete the list of shrimp count sizes.

U/10, U/12, _____, _____, 21/25, _____, _____, _____, _____, _____, 61/70

3. Scallops are classified by count per pound or per half-kilo. Complete the list of scallop count sizes.

U-10, _____, _____, _____, _____, 120-250

4. Name the scallop market form.

_____ Chemical free, no water added.

_____ Packed and shipped within 24 hours of harvest.

_____ Hand harvested.

5. Crabmeat is primarily graded according to color and size of pieces. Complete this list of crabmeat grades, in descending quality order (highest to lowest).

Colossal Lump

_____

_____

_____

_____

_____

Claw fingers

6. Name the caviar type.

_____ Large, separate berries, pale gray to dark gray; rich, mild flavor.

_____ Tiny berries ranging from brown to black; strong, assertive flavor.

_____ Medium-sized berries, golden to brown or brownish-black; nutty flavor.

7. Name the oyster.

_____ Small, delicate oysters introduced to North America's West Coast from Japan.

_____ The only oysters native to North America's West Coast.

_____ Aquacultured oysters originating in Europe; intense, briny flavor and crisp texture.

_____ North America's indigenous East Coast oysters.

_____ Large West Coast oysters originally from Japan.

C. Cold Seafood Procedures

Correctly number the steps in the following procedures and guidelines.

1. Procedure for Poaching Seafood:

_____ Prepare an ice bain-marie.

_____ Cook the seafood just under the desired doneness.

_____ If necessary, fabricate the seafood.

_____ Place the pan in the ice bain-marie.

_____ Bring the *cuisson* to the boil.

_____ Add the seafood to the *cuisson*.

2. Procedure for Preparing Mousses:

_____ Whip the cream.

_____ Place the main ingredient and seasonings in a food processor.

_____ Fold in the whipped cream.

_____ Pack the mousse into its form.

_____ Grind the ingredients into a purée.

_____ Force the purée through a sieve into a large bowl.

3. Procedure for "Cooking" Seafood in Acid:

_____ Prepare the salted, acidic "cooking" liquid.

_____ Monitor the "cooking" time and determine doneness.

_____ Trim and fabricate the raw seafood.

_____ Mix the "cooked" seafood with oil and other seasonings.

_____ Add the raw seafood to the "cooking" liquid.

_____ Drain the seafood.

D. Short-Answer Questions

1. List and describe the three standard *cuissons* that are used for poaching seafood.

   a. _____

   (description) _____

   b. _____

   (description) _____

   c. _____

   (description) _____

2. List four food safety guidelines for handling and serving raw seafood.

   a. _____

   b. _____

   c. _____

   d. _____

3. List and explain the three factors that determine the finished texture of a mousse.

   a. _____

   (explanation) _____

   b. _____

   (explanation) _____

   c. _____

   (explanation) _____

E. Multiple-Choice Questions

1. Which is *not* considered a seafood item?
   a. seaweed
   b. frog's legs
   c. freshwater perch
   d. mussels

2. Which fish egg product is considered a true caviar?
   a. bottarga
   b. sevruga
   c. taramosalata
   d. tobiko

3. Which shellfish item is *not* a bivalve?
   a. clams
   b. shrimp
   c. oysters
   d. mussels

4. Which type of shrimp is best for cold preparations?
   a. tiger shrimp
   b. brown shrimp
   c. canned shrimp
   d. white shrimp

5. Crabmeat is graded according to:
   a. flavor
   b. piece size
   c. color
   d. (a. and c.)
   e. (b. and c.)

6. Seafood for cold service should *not* be cooked by this method:
   a. poaching
   b. pan-frying
   c. grilling
   d. steaming

7. The correct temperature for poaching is:
   a. 120°F (50°C)
   b. 200°F (90°C)
   c. 212°F (100°C)
   d. 350°F (175°C)

8. Which is *not* a classic *cuisson* for poaching seafood?
   a. court bouillon
   b. fish stock
   c. seawater
   d. acidulated water

9. When poaching or steaming seafood, the *wrong* way to manage carryover cooking is:
   a. refreshing
   b. undercooking
   c. pan in ice bain-marie
   d. (b. and c.)

10. Which seafood dish has a "cooked" texture?
    a. ceviche
    b. pesce crudo
    c. sashimi
    d. oysters on the half shell

11. A seafood mousse may be lightened with:
    a. beaten egg whites
    b. whipped cream
    c. gelatin d. (a. and c.)
    d. (a. and b.)

12. True caviar is harvested from:
    a. American sturgeon
    b. Eurasian sturgeon
    c. European carp
    d. Pacific tuna

13. Aquaculture seafood is also referred to as:
    a. farm-raised
    b. free-range
    c. cultivated
    d. (a. and b.)
    e. (a. and c.)

14. Shellfish safety in food service does *not* include:
    a. cooking thoroughly
    b. posting warnings
    c. displaying tags
    d. sanitizing equipment

15. Eggs used in seafood mousses must be:
    a. below 38°F (50°C)
    b. pasteurized
    c. cooked
    d. (b. and c.)

F. Short Essay Questions

1. Discuss steaming as a technique used in preparing cold seafood. Include in your discussion the differences between pan-steaming, stove-top steaming, and pressure steaming. Give an example of the appropriate use of each method.

_____
_____
_____
_____
_____
_____
_____
_____

2. Discuss carryover cooking in poaching seafood to be served cold. Include in your discussion methods of controlling carryover cooking that should and should not be used.

_____

_____

_____

_____

_____

_____

_____

_____

3. Explain the difference between a seafood *mousse* and a seafood *mousseline*.

_____

_____

_____

_____

_____

_____

_____

_____

CHAPTER 7: COLD MEATS

Competent preparation of cold meats and poultry is a requirement for entry-level garde manger work. In addition to being served as dishes in their own right, items such as cold roast beef and poached chicken are key ingredients in other garde manger preparations, most prominently sandwiches and complex salads. Thus, the basic techniques learned in this chapter will be used frequently throughout the text, and in your garde manger career. Skillful presentation of cold meat items is necessary for success in buffet work and for culinary competitions.

Specialty items, such as raw meat dishes, meat-based mousses, and foie gras are hallmarks of advanced garde manger as practiced in high-level restaurants and catering operations. While you may not be asked to work with them early in your career, basic knowledge of them will help you succeed when the challenge arises.

Before studying this chapter, you should already
1. Have read "How to Use This Book," pages xxviii–xxxiii, and understand the professional recipe format.
2. Be familiar with standard cuts of meat and poultry.
3. Know how to determine tenderness or toughness in a cut of meat or poultry.
4. Have mastered basic meat and poultry cooking methods used for hot service.
5. Know how to judge the internal doneness of meat and poultry by both touch and temperature.
6. Know and observe food safety practices for protein-based foods to be served cold.

After reading this chapter, you should be able to
1. Prepare attractive, profitable deli trays.
2. Roast, grill, and poach meats and poultry for cold presentations.
3. Carve roasted meats and poultry correctly and efficiently.
4. Fabricate cold meats and poultry for use in sandwiches, complex salads, and other garde manger preparations.
5. Prepare cold meats and poultry for formal buffet presentations.

A. Key Terms

Fill in each blank with the term that is defined or described.

_____ 1. Can be described as a portable do-it-yourself sandwich station.

_____ 2. The large, intact section of a roast used for presentation.

_____ 3. The term used to describe arranging sliced meats in the order in which they are cut.

_____ 4. Large bundles of greenery placed on the carving board around the base of the roast.

_____ 5. An ornamental skewer used to create height in a platter presentation.

_____ 6. An attractive, composed food item that is self-contained and freestanding on a platter presentation.

_____ 7. The classic, hand-chopped raw beef dish.

_____ 8. A dish composed of thin-sliced raw beef filet.

_____ 9. A spread made from cooked poultry liver puréed with softened butter.

_____ 10. Literally translates as "fat liver."

_____ 11. French term for force-feeding poultry.

_____ 12. A cylindrically formed food item whose shape is achieved by wrapping in plastic film and/or cheesecloth.

_____ 13. A fluid mixture of vegetable oil, an acidic ingredient, salt, and seasonings used to flavor and tenderize meats.

_____ 14. A display at which chefs slice hot or cold meats to order.

_____ 15. French term for raw, unprocessed foie gras.

B. Short-Answer Questions

1. List and describe the three grades of foie gras.

a._____

(description)

_____

54

b._____

(description)

_____

c._____

(description)

_____

2. List two differences between a liver parfait and a liver mousse.

a. _____

b. _____

3. List four food safety guidelines for preparing raw meat dishes.

a. _____

b. _____

c. _____

d. _____

4. Describe the two effects of marination on meats.

a. _____

b. _____

5. List three ways to prevent surface drying on meats and poultry that are served cold.

a. _____

b. _____

c. _____

6. Explain why it is important to highly season foods for cold service.

_____

_____

7. Explain the importance of removing visible fat from meat and poultry dishes for cold service.

_____

_____

C. Cold Meat Procedures

Correctly number the steps in the following procedures and guidelines.
Note: The directions have been condensed and some steps omitted or combined. You must think about the procedures and demonstrate your understanding; do not expect to copy from the text.

1. Procedure for sequencing slices:

_____ Begin slicing across the grain.

_____ Trim surface fat and silverskin.

_____ Determine the direction of the grain.

_____ Arrange the platter, beginning with last slice cut and ending with second slice cut.

_____ Determine the size of the *grosse pièce* and mark it.

_____ Place the slices in order on the board or work tray.

2. Procedure for cleaning and seasoning fresh foie gras:

_____ Slit open the lobes.

_____ Season.

_____ Flush under cool running water.

_____ Pull apart the lobes.

_____ Wrap and place in ice.

_____ Remove visible surface membrane and blemishes.

_____ Use food-service tweezers to remove the veins.

56

3. Procedure for poaching fresh foie gras:

_____ Poach the foie gras *torchon* for the determined time.

_____ Store in cold *cuisson*.

_____ Cool to room temperature in the pan, in an ice bain-marie.

_____ Hold the foie gras *torchon* off the heat in the *cuisson* for the determined time.

_____ Prepare the *torchon*.

_____ Bring the *cuisson* to the simmer.

D. Multiple-Choice Questions

1. In modern food service, cold meats are most frequently used:
   a. for breakfast
   b. as sandwich fillings
   c. as dinner entrées
   d. as gifts

2. When planning a deli tray, your per-person purchasing estimate should be:
   a. 2 oz. meats + 2 oz. cheeses
   b. 5 oz. meats + 3 oz. cheeses
   c. 4 oz. meats + 1 oz. cheeses

3. When carving cold meats, slices should:
   a. be cut with the grain
   b. be cut across the grain
   c. include surface fat
   d. (b. and c.)

4. The classic skewer-like decorative implement used to create height in cold meat platters is:
   a. a *rapier*
   b. an *attelet*
   c. a *pousse-café*
   d. an *hachette*

5. Which is *not* a garniture?
   a. deviled egg
   b. stuffed cherry tomato
   c. tomato rose
   d. mousseline dome

6. For cold service meats should:
   a. have fat removed
   b. be lightly seasoned
   c. be at cool room temperature
   d. d. (b. and c.)

7. For cold service, meats should *not* be cooked by which method?
   a. roasting
   b. grilling
   c. poaching
   d. pan-frying

8. Cold meats have the best mouthfeel and most attractive appearance at an internal doneness of:
   a. rare
   b. medium-rare
   c. medium
   d. medium-well
   e. well-done

9. When determining the internal doneness temperature for cold service, compensate for carryover cooking by subtracting:
   a. 2 to 5°F (5 to 13°C)
   b. 6 to 9°F (16 to 24°C)
   c. 10 to 13°F (26 to 35°C)

10. Poached meats and poultry for cold service are best held refrigerated:
   a. wrapped in aluminum foil
   b. on a rack
   c. submerged in their *cuisson*

11. Steak Tartare may be prepared:
    a. tableside
    b. with a chef's knife
    c. in a meat grinder
    d. (a. and b.)

12. Which is a poor choice for making a meat-based mousse?
    a. beef chuck
    b. chicken breast
    c. smoked ham
    d. duck livers

13. Which ingredient/technique does *not* cause raw red meats to discolor?
    a. advance preparation
    b. lemon juice
    c. olive oil
    d. loose wrapping

E. Short Essay Questions

1. Explain how you would arrange a cold roast turkey platter for buffet service. Include your strategy for portion control, the way in which you would fabricate the meat, the accompaniment(s) you would serve, and how you would decorate the platter.

_____

_____

_____

_____

_____

_____

_____

_____

2. Define *gavage*, describe it, and explain why it is controversial.

_____

_____

_____

_____

_____

_____

_____

3. Write a five-item sandwich menu that features in-house prepared, hand-carved meats and poultry.

_____

_____

_____

_____

_____

CHAPTER 8: COLD SOUPS

Cold soups have a special place in the garde manger repertoire. It is important that you, as a garde manger chef, understand their role in menu planning, and know when it is appropriate to serve them.

Many cold soups begin as hot soups but are chilled before serving. In preparing this type of cold soup you will use the methods and techniques learned in the hot kitchen; however, you must additionally understand the effects of chilling and properly compensate for them. Other cold soups are prepared from raw ingredients and are never heated. Successful preparation of these soups requires proper fabrication of ingredients, careful mixing, and care in adjusting the soups' final consistency.

A frequently faced challenge for the garde manger chef is holding and serving cold soups at the correct temperature. Sourcing or creating the correct equipment is essential.

This chapter gives you the information needed to overcome these challenges and successfully prepare and serve cold soups.

Before studying this chapter, you should already
1. Have read "How to Use This Book," pages xxviii–xxxiii, and understand the professional recipe format.
2. Be proficient at making hot soups.
3. Know the procedure for clarifying stocks, and be proficient at doing so.

After reading this chapter, you should be able to
1. Prepare semisweet and savory cold soups.
2. Identify appropriate ingredients for cold soups.
3. Modify hot soups for cold service.
4. Maintain cold soups at the proper temperature.
5. Serve cold soups at the proper temperature using both purchased and improvised chilling serviceware.
6. Enhance cold soups with interesting and appropriate garnishes and accompaniments.

A. Key Terms

Fill in each blank with the term that is defined or described.

_____ 1. A cold soup with a predominantly sweet flavor typically prepared by the pastry department.

_____ 2. A tiny portion of soup served in a shot glass or demitasse cup as an hors d'oeuvre or amuse-bouche.

_____ 3. A cold, lightly gelatinized soup made from clarified stock.

B. Short-Answer Questions

1. List and define the three categories of cold soups.

a. _____

(definition)_____

b. _____

(definition)_____

c. _____

(definition)_____

2. Why must stocks for use in cold soups be thoroughly defatted?

_____

_____

3. List the six types of cold soup and give an example of each.

a. _____

(example) _____

b. _____

(example) _____

c. _____

(example) _____

d. _____

(example) _____

e. _____

(example) _____

f. _____

(example) _____

4. List three factors that must be taken into account when preparing cold soups, and explain the methods you would use to control them.

a. _____

(method) _____

b. _____

(method) _____

c. _____

(method) _____

5. Suggest three ways to keep a cold soup cold while it is being served and eaten.

a._____

b._____

c._____

C. Know Your Cold Soups

Fill in each blank with the name of the soup that is defined or described.

_____ 1. A semisweet cold soup made by simmering dried fruits in wine.

_____ 2. A soup made with mixed vegetables, tomatoes, dried beans, garlic, olive oil, and pasta; this variation on a hot soup is served cool rather than cold.

_____ 3. A cold soup made with beets, onions, and brown stock, frequently topped with sour cream.

_____ 4. A formal cold soup made with clear, gelatinized brown stock flavored with tomatoes and Madeira.

_____ 5. Of Spanish origin, a rough purée of raw tomatoes, cucumbers, green peppers, garlic, and olive oil.

_____ 6. Popularized at the Ritz-Carlton hotel during the Continental cuisine era, a cold purée of potatoes, leeks, and cream.

_____ 7. The Russian name for a rustic purée of raw cucumbers, yogurt, and buttermilk seasoned with scallions, dill, and garlic.

D. Multiple-Choice Questions

1. Which characteristic is *not* associated with semisweet cold soups?
   a. boldly acidic
   b. served as appetizer
   c. stock-based
   d. little or no added sugar

2. Which ingredient is appropriate for use in cold soups?
   a. bacon drippings
   b. walnut oil
   c. blonde roux
   d. maître d' hotel butter

3. Which vessel is *not* appropriate for serving cold soups?
   a. shrimp cocktail chiller
   b. bread bowl
   c. soup cup set in bowl of ice
   d. shot glass

4. To achieve a smooth texture in cold soups, you can use:
   a. a food mill
   b. an immersion blender
   c. mesh sieve
   d. (a., b., and c.)

5. If a soup normally served hot is to be served cold, you should decrease the thickening ingredient(s) by about:

    a. 10%

    b. 20%

    c. 30%

    d. 40%

6. Which is/are *not* recommended for seasoning soups that are cold?

    a. fine sea salt

    b. iodized table salt

    c. coarse kosher salt

    d. (b. and c.)

E. Short Essay Questions

1. Recount the history of cold soups and discuss their role in modern menu planning.

_____

_____

_____

_____

_____

_____

_____

2. A member of your culinary team has prepared a cold soup having two major flaws: it is too thick, and it tastes flat. What would you advise him or her to do?

_____

_____

_____

_____

_____

_____

_____

3. You have been asked to prepare a flight of three cold soup sips as the first course of a special dinner. List and describe the soups you would serve, and justify your choices.

Sip #1: _____

(description) _____

Sip #2: _____

(description) _____

Sip #3: _____

(description) _____

I chose this combination because: _____

_____

_____

_____

_____

_____

CHAPTER 9: GARDE MANGER SANDWICHES

Because sandwiches are commonplace foods, chefs sometimes forget to adequately train their staffs in proper sandwich-making techniques and leave the preparation to chance. This is a mistake because sandwiches are popular items that can be quite profitable. Serving consistently good sandwiches can build your operation's reputation and lead to increased sales.

This chapter enables you to think about the many types of sandwiches in an organized way. Once you master construction of the various types of sandwich, you can develop new sandwiches of your own creation. You will also learn to set up and maintain a well-organized sandwich station, enabling you to make sandwiches quickly and efficiently.

Before studying this chapter, you should already
1. Have read "How to Use This Book," pp. xxviii–xxxiii, and understand the professional recipe format.
2. Have mastered the preparation of bound protein salads covered in Chapter 5.
3. Have mastered the preparation of cold meats and poultry covered in Chapter 7.
4. Know basic sanitation procedures for products served raw.
5. Know state and local regulations for food-service glove use.

After reading this chapter, you should be able to
1. Name the four elements of a basic sandwich, and explain the functions of each.
2. List and describe the six basic sandwich construction types and explain the principles of sandwich construction.
3. Properly use the tools and equipment found in a modern sandwich station.
4. Become proficient at both plated and tray presentation of sandwiches.
5. Correctly package sandwiches for box lunches and to-go service.
6. Set up and maintain an efficient sandwich station.
7. Correctly prepare the most popular North American cold sandwiches as well as the hot sandwiches typically prepared in the garde manger station.
8. Combine food items and ingredients to make successful new sandwich creations.

A. Key Terms

Fill in each blank with the term that is defined or described.

_____ 1. Light-textured breads made with yeast.

_____ 2. The soft, porous interior of a leavened bread.

_____ 3. The exterior of a leavened bread.

_____ 4. Breads that do not contain yeast and therefore do not rise.

_____ 5. Breads that contain yeast but that are fabricated so as to have very little rise.

_____ 6. A liquid or paste-like dressing usually applied to the bread element of a sandwich.

_____ 7. Butter flavored with various seasonings, condiments, or other ingredients.

_____ 8. A piece of food included in a sandwich presentation in order to enhance the sandwich and that is served outside the sandwich rather than included inside it.

_____ 9. Breads made in small batches, by traditional processes, and from natural ingredients.

_____ 10. An enhancing element included inside a sandwich.

_____ 11. An Italian-style pressed sandwich.

_____ 12. A pressed sandwich invented in Florida by immigrants from a Caribbean island.

B. Sandwich Types

Fill in each blank with the name of the sandwich type that is defined or described.

_____ 1. Fillings and internal garnishes between three bread slices.

_____ 2. Examples are hoagies, subs, and heros.

_____ 3. Sandwiches simultaneously toasted and flattened between two iron plates.

_____ 4. Filing(s) and internal garnishes rolled into a flatbread.

_____ 5. Filling(s) warmed in an oven or microwave and then encased in a bread product.

_____ 6. Filling(s) and internal garnishes between two bread slices or in a split round roll.

_____ 7. Assembled sandwiches warmed in an oven.

_____ 8. Visible fillings and garnishes arranged on one slice of bread.

_____ 9. Filling(s) and internal garnishes inside an opened pita-type bread.

68

C. Short-Answer Questions

1. List the four basic elements of a sandwich.

a._____   c._____

b._____   d._____

2. List six examples of sandwich spreads.

a._____   d._____

b._____   e._____

c._____   f._____

3. Name the three qualities that properly cooked bacon adds to a cold sandwich.

a._____

b._____

c._____

4. Give three examples of an external sandwich garnish.

a._____

b._____

c._____

5. Give three examples of an internal sandwich garnish.

a._____

b._____

c._____

6. List the six basic sandwich construction types, and give an example of each.

a._____

(example)_____

b._____

(example)_____

c._____

(example)_____

d._____

(example)_____

e._____

(example)_____

f._____

(example)_____

D. Know Your Sandwiches

Fill in each blank with the name of the sandwich that is defined or described.

_____ 1. A pressed sandwich consisting of smoked ham, roast pork, Swiss cheese, pickles, and mustard on a wide long roll.

_____ 2. A simple sandwich consisting of corned beef, Russian dressing, and cole slaw on rye.

_____ 3. A double-decker sandwich consisting of bacon, lettuce, tomato, and turkey breast with mayonnaise on toasted white bread.

_____ 4. A pressed sandwich consisting of smoked ham and Gruyère cheese on firm white bread.

_____ 5. A hollowed long roll sandwich consisting of ham, salami, provolone cheese, lettuce, tomato, and onion traditionally moistened with an Italian-style dressing.

_____ 6. A toasted frankfurter roll filled with lobster salad .

_____ 7. A toasted sandwich consisting of tuna salad, mustard, Swiss cheese, lettuce, and tomato.

70

E. Multiple-Choice Questions

1. Bread products for sandwiches must be:
    a. sturdy
    b. tender
    c. correctly fabricated
    d. (a. and c.)
    e. (a., b., and c.)

2. Which is *not* an appropriate bread for wrap sandwiches?
    a. whole wheat flour tortillas
    b. lavash
    c. focaccia
    d. flour tortillas

3. Breads and rolls for sandwiches should *not* be stored:
    a. in micro-perforated bag at room temperature
    b. in plastic film in refrigerator
    c. in plastic bag in freezer

4. The portion size of a sandwich is expressed as the weight of:
    a. the main filling item only
    b. the main filling item plus cheese
    c. all ingredients except the bread
    d. the weight of the entire sandwich

5. The sandwich was widely popularized in eighteenth-century:
    a. United States
    b. Australia
    c. Canada
    d. Great Britain

6. Which is *not* one of the four basic sandwich elements?
    a. external garnish
    b. spread
    c. bread
    d. filling
    e. internal garnish

7. Frozen bread products should be thawed:
    a. wrapped, room temperature
    b. unwrapped, room temperature
    c. wrapped, refrigerated

8. Which is *not* an advantage of using house-made sandwich meats and poultry?
   a. customer perceives quality
   b. can utilize leftovers
   c. unique items
   d. low labor cost

9. Which is *not* a good idea for setting up a sandwich station?
   a. pre-slicing bread
   b. assembling sandwiches
   c. portioning fillings
   d. filling squeeze bottles

10. In addition to a sandwich, a typical box lunch contains:
    a. a soft drink
    b. a piece of fruit
    c. a cookie
    d. (a. and c.)
    e. (a., b., and c.)

F. Short Essay Questions

1. From your own experience, describe the qualities of a well-made sandwich. Include in your discussion the qualities of appearance, flavor, mouthfeel, ease of eating, and value.

_____
_____
_____
_____
_____

2. Create a five-item sandwich menu, and justify your choices.

_____
_____
_____
_____

I chose these items because: _____
_____
_____
_____

3. On a separate piece of paper, draw a station map (p. 14) for your menu. On your map, show the direction of flow when sandwiches are made.

CHAPTER 10: COLD HORS D'OEUVRES

The preparation of hors d'oeuvres allows garde manger chefs to showcase their creativity. Virtually any savory food can be transformed into an hors d'oeuvre. However, in order to present an attractive selection of successful hors d'oeuvres, you must understand hors d'oeuvre construction. Knowing the five basic hors d'oeuvre types presented in this chapter enables you to develop a varied menu. Using the proper assembly methods makes hors d'oeuvre production faster and easier. Finally, following the rules of hors d'oeuvre presentation results in efficient service and increased customer satisfaction.

Before studying this chapter, you should already
1. Understand the professional recipe format outlined in "How To Use This Book," pp. xxviii–xxxiii.
2. Be proficient in preparing the cold meats, cold seafood, cold vegetables, and complex salads that are components of many hors d'oeuvres.

After reading this chapter, you should be able to
1. List the six requirements for successful hors d'oeuvres.
2. Identify foods frequently used for hors d'oeuvre preparations.
3. List and describe the five basic construction types of hors d'oeuvres.
4. Prepare a variety of cold hors d'oeuvres.
5. List and explain the four elements of hors d'oeuvre tray design.
6. Present hors d'oeuvres attractively on various types of serviceware.

A. Key Terms
Fill in each blank with the term that is defined or described.

_____ 1. A small, attractive piece of savory food meant to be picked up and eaten with the fingers.

_____ 2. The type of service in which trays of hors d'oeuvres are placed on tables.

_____ 3. An hors d'oeuvre that consists of a small piece of food filled with a complementary food item or preparation.

_____ 4. A type of service in which trays of hors d'oeuvres are carried from person to person by servers.

_____ 5. An hors d'oeuvre that consists of foods layered together and then rolled into a cylinder.

_____ 6. A contemporary hors d'oeuvre style in which a small portion of food is served on a spoon.

_____ 7. An alcohol beverage originally consisting of a spirit mixed with a non-alcohol beverage such as carbonated water.

_____ 8. A contemporary hors d'oeuvre style consisting of a hot or cold soup presented in a shot glass or demitasse cup.

_____ 9. A food item added to a tray or platter to add visual appeal.

_____ 10. An hors d'oeuvre consisting of two or three pieces of food threaded on a skewer.

_____ 11. Examples are barquettes, tartlets, bouchées, and mini-profiteroles.

_____ 12. Raw or very lightly cooked vegetables served chilled and accompanied by various dips.

_____ 13. Hors d'oeuvres that are cooked ahead, then reheated prior to serving.

_____ 14. Large, perfect leaves of lettuce, kale, and other leafy vegetables used to line trays for cold hors d'oeuvres.

_____ 15. An hors d'oeuvre that can be described as a miniature open-face sandwich.

_____ 16. A drink based on table wine or a fortified wine such as sherry or vermouth.

_____ 17. The French term for "finger food."

_____ 18. The term used to describe a pastry shell that is baked without a filling.

_____ 19. Tools for punching out small, decorative shapes.

_____ 20. An hors d'oeuvre consisting of a small piece of food impaled on a cocktail pick.

B. Short-Answer Questions

1. List the four elements of hors d'oeuvre presentation and describe the role each plays in the overall presentation.

a._____

(description)_____

b._____

(description)_____

c._____

(description)_____

d._____

(description)_____

2. List the six characteristics of a successful hors d'oeuvre.

a._____

b._____

c._____

d._____

e._____

f._____

3. List five food items that can be stuffed as cold hors d'oeuvres.

a._____   d._____

b._____   e._____

c._____

4. List five food items that can be used to make rolled hors d'oeuvres.

a._____   d._____
b._____   e._____
c._____

5. List five food items that can be used to make skewered hors d'oeuvres.

a._____   d._____
b._____   e._____
c._____

6. List five examples of pastry hors d'oeuvres.

a._____   d._____
b._____   e._____
c._____

7. Name the three basic elements of a canapé.

a._____   b._____   c._____

8. Explain why it is important to use a ruler for canapé production.

_____

_____

9. Name and describe the two basic methods for constructing canapés.

a._____

(description)_____

_____

b._____

(description)_____

_____

10. List five pastry doughs frequently used in making hors d'oeuvres.

a._____ d._____

b._____ e._____

c._____

C. Canapé Production Procedures

Correctly number the steps in the following procedures and guidelines.
Note: The directions have been condensed and some steps omitted or combined. You must think about the procedures and demonstrate your understanding; do not expect to copy from the text.

1. Procedure for constructing canapés by the slab method:

_____ Apply a thin, even layer of spread to the bread slabs.

_____ Apply the filling to the slabs in a thin, even layer.

_____ Refrigerate the slabs until the spread has firmed up enough to cut.

_____ Using a sharp chef knife, trim the slabs into even rectangles, then use a ruler to cut even-sized pieces.

_____ Transfer the canapés to a sheet tray lined with parchment.

_____ Apply garnishes using the production line method.

_____ Prepare bread slabs.

2. Procedure for constructing canapés by the individual method:

_____ Apply the garnishes to the canapés using the production line method.

_____ Apply a thin, even layer of spread to each individual canapé base.

_____ Prepare bread bases.

_____ Pre-cut or size the filling items to fit the bases.

_____ Place each base on a parchment-lined sheet tray as it is completed.

_____ Apply the filling to each individual canapé base.

D. Multiple-Choice Questions

1. Passed hors d'oeuvres are associated with:
    a. banquet service
    b. butler service
    c. buffet service
    d. room service

2. Which is *not* a characteristic of a properly prepared hors d'oeuvre?
    a. small
    b. neat and self-contained
    c. subtly seasoned
    d. attractive

3. An alternate term for a rolled hors d'oeuvre:
    a. rumaki
    b. roulade
    c. rillette
    d. rechaud

4. Which is *not* a pastry hors d'oeuvre?
    a. chausson
    b. bouchée
    c. barquette
    d. galantine

5. Canapés that feature smoked salmon and caviar should be made by the:
    a. slab method
    b. well method
    c. flaky pastry method
    d. individual method

6. Which is *not* appropriate as a liner for a pastry hors d'oeuvre tray?
    a. Romaine lettuce leaves
    b. greaseproof doily
    c. linen napkin
    d. colored paper doily

7. Which vessel is *not* appropriate for butler service?
   a. silver platter
   b. flat basket
   c. lacquerware tray
   d. glass serving plate

8. Successful tray décor:
   a. adds height
   b. adds color
   c. supports a theme
   d. (a. and b.)
   e. (a., b., and c.)

9. An apèritif may include:
   a. rum
   b. brandy
   c. vermouth
   d. club soda
   e. (c. and d.)

10. Hors d'oeuvres are *not* served:

   a. with dinner
   b. at receptions
   c. before dinner
   d. at cocktail parties

E. Short Essay Questions

1. Explain how the term "hors d'oeuvre" is used differently in Europe than in North America.

_____

_____

_____

_____

_____

_____

2. Explain the importance of choosing the correct serviceware when presenting hors d'oeuvres.

_____

_____

_____

_____

_____

_____

_____

3. Design a cocktail party menu consisting of six different hors d'oeuvres and justify your choices.

a. (menu item) _____

(description)_____

b. (menu item) _____

(description)_____

c. (menu item) _____

(description)_____

d. (menu item) _____

(description)_____

e. (menu item) _____

(description)_____

f. (menu item) _____

(description)_____

CHAPTER 11: CURED AND SMOKED FOODS

Curing and smoking are among the most complex and technical of all garde manger procedures. Producing high quality cured and smoked products requires thorough understanding of the scientific principles explained in this chapter. Producing cured foods that are safe for your customers to eat requires attention to detail and a serious attitude. To produce wholesome products, practice careful measurement, strict adherence to proper procedures, acute observation when evaluating products, and meticulous sanitation. Make sure that you can correctly answer the questions in this workbook chapter before attempting to prepare cured and smoked foods.

Before studying this chapter, you should already
1. Have read "How to Use This Book," pp. xxviii–xxxiii, and understand the professional recipe format.
2. Know how to accurately scale up and scale down recipe formula amounts.
3. Know how to accurately weigh ingredients using both a spring scale and a digital scale.
4. Be able to correctly fabricate various cuts of meat, poultry, and seafood.
5. Be able to create and maintain accurate records of the times and temperatures involved in food production.

After you read this chapter, you should be able to
1. Explain the scientific principles involved in curing foods.
2. Prepare the two basic types of curing compounds, and use nitrite/nitrate curing mixes safely and effectively.
3. Identify appropriate meats, poultry, and seafood for curing, and choose the most appropriate curing compounds for each.
4. Use both the dry cure and brine cure methods to cure meats, poultry, and seafood.
5. Describe the results that occur when wood smoke is applied to cured foods.
6. Explain the science of smoking.
7. Select smoking equipment appropriate for your operation's product list, sales volume, and budget.
8. Prepare smoked products by both the hot smoking and cold smoking methods.
9. Prepare various types of confit and other traditional and modern foods sealed in fat.

A. Key Terms
Fill in each blank with the term that is defined or described.

_____ 1. General term for any mixture of salt, sugar, spices, and herbs used in preserving meats.

_____ 2. To treat a food with salt, making it less hospitable to bacteria, and thus delaying spoilage.

_____ 3. Transference of fluids through cell wall membranes.

_____ 4. A preserving mixture based on dry salt and other dry ingredients in granular or powdered form.

_____ 5. Another name for a dry cure.

_____ 6. Term for the liquid that results when salt is dissolved in water.

_____ 7. A preserving mixture consisting of water, salt, and seasonings.

_____ 8. A brine cure that has a strong acidic component, today most commonly associated with preserved vegetables.

_____ 9. A brine that is heated in order to dissolve the salt and extract the flavors of whole spices and aromatics.

_____ 10. Old-fashioned term for applying a cure; today used to describe brine curing of beef.

_____ 11. Salts that undergo a manufacturing process removing all minerals other than sodium chloride.

_____ 12. Salts that contain various other minerals in addition to sodium chloride.

_____ 13. A refined salt processed into flaky particles that dissolve quickly and penetrate evenly.

_____ 14. An unrefined, natural salt made by evaporating seawater.

_____ 15. The chemical compound $NaNO_2$, used widely in meat preservation.

_____ 16. The chemical compound $NaNO_3$, used less frequently in meat preservation.

_____ 17. General term used for nitrite/salt mixtures colored pink with red food coloring.

_____ 18. This mixture contains 6% sodium nitrite and 94% sodium chloride plus a small amount of red food coloring.

_____ 19. 6% sodium nitrite, 94% sodium chloride, red food coloring, and a fraction of a percent of sodium nitrate.

_____ 20. A potentially hazardous substance that is formed when foods containing nitrites or nitrates are subjected to high heat.

_____ 21. Ingredients used to help the curing compound penetrate into meats more quickly as well as aid in flavor and color development.

_____ 22. General term for substances used to aid in retaining moisture in cured foods.

_____ 23. The translucent, tacky skin that forms on air-dried cured products.

_____ 24. A procedure in which a food item to be cured is placed in a container and immersed in a wet curing mixture.

_____ 25. General term for a wet cure applied to both the exterior and interior of the meat.

_____ 26. A technique that involves forcing brine through a needle directly into the muscle structure of the meat.

_____ 27. A technique in which brine is forced into the large blood vessels in a front leg or hind leg primal cut.

_____ 28. General term for a tool used for forcing brine into meat .

_____ 29. A procedure done to dry-cured meat that involves periodically turning it and rotating its position in the curing tub.

_____ 30. In a smoker, the enclosed area where meat is placed and in which smoke is trapped.

_____ 31. Wood stored for at least a year after harvest.

_____ 32. The type of smoking in which foods are held at temperatures below 100°F during the application of smoke.

_____ 33. The type of smoking in which foods are surrounded by smoke at temperatures between 150–200°F (65°C–93°C).

_____ 34. The process by which animal fats are melted and released from their surrounding connective tissue.

_____ 35. Foods that are first cured and then cooked and sealed in fat.

_____ 36. Meats cooked in a flavorful, fatty liquid, shredded, and then sealed in fat.

B. Short-Answer Questions

1. List and describe the four phases of the curing process.

a._____

(description)

_____

b._____

(description)

_____

c._____

(description)

_____

d._____

(description)

_____

2. List the four functions of the pellicle.

a._____

b._____

c._____

d._____

3. List five woods typically used for smoking.

a._____   d._____

b._____   e._____

c._____

4. List five flavoring ingredients that may be used to flavor smoked foods.

a._____   d._____

b._____   e._____

c._____

5. List three garde manger products that are/may be sealed in fat.

a._____   c._____

b._____

C. Procedures

Correctly number the steps in the following procedures and guidelines.
Note: The directions have been condensed and some steps omitted or combined. You must think about the procedures and demonstrate your understanding; do not expect to copy from the text.

1. Procedure for Immersion Brining:

_____ When the pellicle has formed, wrap the food or proceed with additional processing.

_____ Mix the salt, cool water and other brine ingredients in a sanitized container.

_____ Refrigerate the meat in the brine for the time specified in the recipe.

_____ Fabricate the meat as specified in the recipe.

_____ Place the meat in the brine and, if necessary, weight it down with a plate.

_____ Test the cure.

_____ Drain and air-dry the meat.

2. Procedure for Dry Curing:

_____ Fabricate the meat to be cured.

_____ Cure the meat according to the specified time and temperature.

_____ Prepare the dry cure compound.

_____ After the pellicle has formed, wrap the food or proceed with additional processing.

_____ Massage an even layer of dry cure compound onto all surfaces of the meat.

_____ Test the cure.

_____ When curing is complete, brush or wash any remaining dry cure compound off the meat's surface.

_____ Air-dry the meat.

3. Procedure for Smoking:

_____ Air-dry the cured food to form the pellicle.

_____ After smoking is complete, air-dry the smoked product.

_____ Turn on the heat source and allow smoke to build in the smoking chamber.

_____ Fabricate and cure the food to be smoked.

_____ Place the prepared wood for smoking on the heat source.

_____ Place the cured food in the smoking chamber and close the door.

_____ Set a timer for maintenance and smoke the meat for the specified time.

_____ Wrap the smoked product(s) in butcher paper and refrigerate.

4. Procedure for Making Confit:

_____ Pour or ladle the hot fat over the meat.

_____ Fabricate and cure the meat.

_____ Melt the semi-solid fat on the stovetop in a brazier.

_____ Rinse the curing compound off of the meat and blot it dry.

_____ Cook the meat on the stovetop or bake it in the oven until the meat is very tender.

_____ Place the confit in the refrigerator and allow to mellow for one week.

_____ When the fat reaches 200°F (93°C) place the meat into it, making sure all pieces are submerged.

_____ Transfer the meat to a sanitized container.

_____ Open-pan cool the confit to room temperature.

D. Multiple-Choice Questions

1. After curing, meats have:
   a. firmer, denser texture
   b. saltier flavor
   c. higher bacteria count
   d. (a. and c.)
   e. (a. and b.)

2. A dry cure is also called a/an:
   a. pickle
   b. brine
   c. overhaul
   d. rub

3. A dry cure *must* contain:
   a. sugar
   b. spices
   c. a TCM
   d. salt
   e. (c. and d.)

4. In addition to water, a brine *must* contain:
   a. spices
   b. a TCM
   c. salt
   d. (a. and b.)
   e. (b. and c.)

5. Which should *not* be used for curing?
   a. fine-grind table salt
   b. kosher salt
   c. medium-grind sea salt
   d. (a. and c.)

6. If your recipe specifies Prague Powder #1, but you don't have any:
   a. you can substitute a cure accelerator, such as ascorbic acid.
   b. you can leave it out, realizing that your product won't keep as long.
   c. you can substitute Prague Powder #2.
   d. you should not proceed to make the product.

7. In cured products, sugar contributes:
    a. moist mouthfeel
    b. pink color
    c. balanced flavor
    d. (a. and b.)
    e. (b. and c.)

8. Which is *not* appropriate for curing?
    a. fresh ham
    b. salmon side
    c. duck legs
    d. filet of beef
    e. pork belly

9. Which 2 lb. (1 kg) item requires the *least* amount of curing compound?
    a. salmon side
    b. boneless pork shoulder
    c. pork belly
    d. beef brisket

10. Which is *not* a safe vessel to use for dry curing?
    a. bus tub
    b. stainless steel saucepan
    c. hotel pan
    d. aluminum saucepan
    e. (b. and d.)

11. Which can successfully be cured by immersion brining, with no internal brining?
    a. fresh ham
    b. boneless trout
    c. pork shoulder
    d. whole turkey

12. Which cured product is ready to eat after curing, with no further cooking?
    a. salt cod
    b. gravlax
    c. bacon
    d. corned beef

13. The presentation of cold-smoked foods is characterized by:
  a. thin slicing
  b. re-heating
  c. thick slicing
  d. (b. and c.)
  e. (a. and b.)

14. It is *not* safe to operate an electric smoker:
  a. under a commercial exhaust system
  b. outdoors, on a covered loading dock
  c. in an air-conditioned food storage area
  d. outdoors, under a picnic pavilion

15. Confits are preserved by:
  a. curing
  b. sealing in fat
  c. smoking
  d. (a. and b.)
  e. (b. and c.)

16. Rillettes are preserved by:
  a. curing
  b. sealing in fat
  c. smoking
  d. (a. and b.)
  e. (b. and c.)

17. The abbreviation commonly used for pink-colored curing compounds is:
  a. PCC
  b. TNC
  c. TCM
  d. NCC

E. Short Essay Questions

1. Explain the science of curing. How does salt preserve foods?

_____

_____

_____

2. Demonstrate your understanding of nitrite/nitrate curing mixes.

Why are they tinted pink? _____

What is the difference between the two types? _____

_____

_____

What safety precautions must you take when working with them? _____

_____

_____

_____

Explain the controversy over their use, and how you would reassure your customers about the safety of your products containing them. _____

_____

_____

_____

_____

3. Demonstrate your understanding of the smoking process.

What are the two types of smoking as defined by temperature, and what are their effects on foods?

a. _____

_____

_____

b. _____

_____

_____

Why are foods always cured before smoking? _____

_____

_____

_____

CHAPTER 12: SAUSAGES

This chapter introduces forcemeats, a fundamental element of many charcuterie specialties. Although these mixtures of ground meat, fat, and seasonings appear to be relatively simple, in fact their correct preparation is quite complex and demanding. To produce successful forcemeats, you must understand scientific principles such as emulsification and protein development. Many sausage forcemeats include cures and TCMs that must be measured with care. You must pay strict attention to ingredient temperatures and cooking times. You must closely observe your product from start to finish and know how to correct problems as they arise. Because the information presented in this chapter pertains to the pâté and terrine forcemeats in Chapter 13, you must master it before you move ahead.

In addition to preparing sausage forcemeats, to make most types of sausage you must also learn the techniques involved in encasement. Choosing the proper casings, preparing them, and filling them requires manual skill and sound judgment. Finally, many sausage types require some type of finishing that draws on your previously acquired knowledge of poaching, steaming, and smoking. Test your readiness for sausage preparation by correctly answering the questions in this workbook chapter and reviewing your answers in workbook Chapter 11.

Before studying this chapter, you should already
1. Have read "How to Use This Book," pages xxviii–xxxiii, and understand the professional recipe format.
2. Have read Chapter 11, "Cured and Smoked Foods," and have achieved a thorough understanding of salt curing (p. 410) and nitrite/nitrate curing mixes (p. 412).
3. Be able to identify primal meat cuts and have mastered basic meat fabrication.

After reading this chapter, you should be able to
1. List and describe the four basic types of ground meat sausages and the two basic types of emulsified sausages.
2. Correctly and safely use meat grinders, planetary mixers, food processors, and sausage stuffers.
3. Prepare sausage products according to food safety guidelines.
4. Successfully prepare ground meat forcemeats and puréed forcemeats.
5. Use various types of natural and manufactured casings to prepare encased sausages.
6. Finish sausages by poaching and hot smoking, cold smoking, and drying.

A. Key Terms
Fill in each blank with the term that is defined or described.

_____ 1. A mixture of seasoned ground meat and ground fat.

_____ 2. A mixture of highly seasoned ground meat and fat blended together in a special way to create both a protein bind and an emulsion.

_____ 3. The inner lining of the intestines and other parts of the digestive tract of various meat animals.

_____ 4. Long, flexible tubes that encase or surround the forcemeat of most sausage products.

_____ 5. Small cubes or pieces of food that are mixed into the ground forcemeat of a sausage.

_____ 6. A thin, tender membrane with a lacy pattern of fat that surrounds the stomach and intestines of hogs and sheep.

_____ 7. Type of sausage made from forcemeat ground to varying degrees of fineness or coarseness in a meat grinder.

_____ 8. Type of sausage made from forcemeats that are puréed to a smooth texture.

_____ 9. Type of sausage intended to be cooked and consumed within a day or two of production, or frozen.

_____ 10. Type of sausage preserved with a curing compound and air-dried; these sausages have a smooth texture and concentrated flavor and are eaten as is with no cooking.

_____ 11. Cured and dried sausages that contain a beneficial bacterial culture.

_____ 12. Cured and dried sausages that are smoked at a temperature below 100°F (37°C).

_____ 13. Sausages that are cured then smoked at a temperature between 170°F (76°C) and 200°F (93°C).

_____ 14. Type of emulsified sausage that does *not* contain a nitrite/nitrate curing mix.

_____ 15. To tenderize meat by grinding and puréeing, without the action heat or acids.

_____ 16. Pork that has been frozen for a time-temperature period proven to destroy the pathogens that can cause trichinosis.

_____ 17. The layer of fat deposited between the back muscles of a hog and its skin.

_____ 18. Type of emulsified sausage that is hot smoked, poached, and contains a nitrite/nitrate curing mix.

_____ 19. The dense, pure white deposit fat located in the hog's head.

_____ 20. Fatback preserved with salt.

_____ 21. The deposit fat that forms around an animal's kidney.

_____ 22. Another name for the skin on a pork slab.

_____ 23. Fat deposited between the various muscles in the animal's body.

_____ 24. Product that is the result of rendering suet.

_____ 25. Deposit fat that forms around an animal's kidney.

_____ 26. A powdered glucose sweetener, which is often added to sausage forcemeats.

_____ 27. A product that reproduces the flavors produced by the action of bacteria in traditionally fermented sausages.

_____ 28. Type of bacterial culture used to lower the pH when added to sausage.

_____ 29. Type of casings manufactured from the protein substance found in the skin, flesh, and connective tissue of animals.

_____ 30. Traditional term for a bundle of casings.

_____ 31. Casings made from plastic or from plant fiber.

_____ 32. A grinder plate that has multiple openings of a particular shape and size.

_____ 33. A mixer that both revolves and rotates.

_____ 34. A machine that works by spinning meat and other foods in a horizontal circular motion that brings the meat into periodic contact with vertically rotating blades.

_____ 35. A machine that pushes forcemeat into casings.

_____ 36. A tube onto which sausage casings are threaded.

_____ 37. Adding salt, herbs, and spices to meats before grinding.

_____ 38. A tool used to puncture holes in the casing of a filled sausage in order to prevent bursting during cooking.

_____ 39. The combined weight of the meat and fat in a forcemeat.

_____ 40. Traditional emulsified sausage formula.

_____ 41. Term for the result of mixing, in which separate particles of meat and fat bond together in a network and create a smooth, cohesive mass.

_____ 42. Additional ingredients added to a forcemeat to help the meat and fat bind together and to stabilize the emulsion.

_____ 43. Cooking and tasting a small sample of forcemeat to determine if any corrections must be made.

_____ 44. The process of stuffing a forcemeat into a casing.

_____ 45. An enclosed area in which sausages are kept under correct conditions for drying.

_____ 46. Occurs when a sausage drying environment is too dry; causes internal spoilage.

B. Short-Answer Questions

1. List the six functions of sausage casings.

a._____

b._____

c._____

d._____

e._____

f._____

2. List and describe the four phases of sausage preparation.

a._____

(description)

_____

b._____

(description)

_____

c._____

(description)

_____

d._____

(description)

_____

3. Explain the function(s) of the following sausage ingredients and, where appropriate, discuss ratios.

a. Functions of fat:

1._____

2._____

Minimum ratio _____% lean meat to _____% fat

Maximum ratio _____% lean meat to _____% fat

b. Function of liquid:

_____

Which type of sausage has the highest liquid to solids ratio? _____

c. Functions of salt:

1. _____

2. _____

4. List three ways to maintain proper forcemeat temperature.

a._____

b._____

c._____

5. Give three examples of a secondary binder.

a._____

b._____

c._____

6. Give two examples of each sausage type.

a. Fresh sausages: _____ and _____

b. Fermented sausages: _____ and _____

c. Cured and hot smoked sausages: _____ and _____

d. Cured and dried sausages: _____ and _____

e. Cured and cold smoked sausages: _____ and _____

f. White emulsified sausages: _____ and _____

g. Cured and smoked emulsified sausages: _____ and _____

7. List five ingredients that can be used as internal garnishes for sausage.

a._____

b._____

c._____

d._____

e._____

8. List the four main reasons why natural casings are preferred by charcutiers.

a. _____

b. _____

c. _____

d. _____

9. List the six basic methods for finishing sausages.

a._____

b._____

c._____

d._____

e._____

f._____

10. List the four conditions necessary to properly dry sausages. Indicate the two that are most important.

a._____

b._____

c._____

d._____

C. Procedures

Correctly number the steps in the following procedures and guidelines.

Note: The directions have been condensed and some steps omitted or combined. You must think about the procedures and demonstrate your understanding; do not expect to copy from the text.

1. General procedure for making standard-grind forcemeats:

_____ If necessary, adjust the formula.

_____ Perform a poach test.

_____ Proceed with further processing, or refrigerate immediately.

_____ Transfer the ground meat mixture to a mixer fitted with an ice bain-marie.

_____ Mix on moderate speed, add cold liquid ingredients in a slow stream to build the emulsion.

_____ Grind the forcemeat ingredients as indicated in the recipe.

_____ Mix in any internal garnishes.

_____ Fabricate all fats and lean meats to fit the grinder, season, and refrigerate.

2. Procedure for encasing sausages:

_____ Shape the lengths as desired.

_____ Cut, flush, and soak the casings.

_____ Fill the sausage stuffer chamber with forcemeat, attach the horn, and lubricate it.

_____ Fill the casing.

_____ Sanitize and chill the sausage stuffing equipment and tools.

_____ Proceed with further processing, or refrigerate.

_____ Thread a length of casing onto the horn.

_____ Fabricate the sausages into desired length and tie off.

_____ Prick with teasing needle.

D. Multiple-Choice Questions

1. Highly seasoned, thoroughly mixed ground meat and fat is called:
    a. a *farce*
    b. a forcemeat
    c. bulk sausage
    d. (a. and b.)
    e. (a., b., and c.)

2. Artisan charcutiers prefer:
    a. manufactured casings
    b. natural casings
    c. no casings
    d. collagen casings

3. Which is *not* an appropriate internal garnish for sausage?
    a. diced apples
    b. pistachio nuts
    c. parsley sprig
    d. diced fatback

4. Which sausage type is *never* eaten as is, with no further cooking?
    a. cured and dried
    b. fermented
    c. fresh
    d. cured and hot smoked

5. Which is *not* a characteristic of an emulsified sausage?
    a. smooth texture
    b. needs no cooking
    c. perishable
    d. easy to make

6. Which is an appropriate meat for sausage making?
    a. pork shoulder
    b. beef tenderloin
    c. chicken breast
    d. veal top round

7. Pork for making cured-and-dried sausages should be:
    a. frozen at 5°F (-15°C) for 20 days
    b. free-range
    c. certified
    d. (a. and b.)
    e. (a. and c.)

8. The preferred fat for sausage making is:
    a. duck fat
    b. butter
    c. lamb fat
    d. pork fat

9. Products that add sweetness and moist mouthfeel to sausages include:
    a. lactose
    b. bellicose
    c. dextrose
    d. comatose

10. Which makes the smallest-diameter sausage?
    a. sheep casings
    b. hog casings
    c. beef middles
    d. hog bungs

11. You must wear food-service gloves when preparing this type of sausage for retail sales:
    a. emulsified
    b. cured and hot smoked
    c. fresh
    d. (a., b., and c.)

12. Forcemeats for standard-grind sausages can be made in a:
    a. food processor
    b. free-standing grinder
    c. mixer grinder attachment
    d. (a. and b.)
    e. (b. and c.)

13. Emulsified sausage forcemeats can be made in a:
    a. food processor
    b. rotation chopper
    c. mixer grinder attachment
    d. (a. and b.)
    e. (b. and c.)

14. Before proceeding to grind meat and fat for forcemeats, the grinder parts must be:
    a. at room temperature
    b. moistened
    c. chilled
    d. oiled

15. A cooked sausage that tastes dry and grainy is likely the result of:
    a. too much fat in the formula
    b. too little fat in the formula
    c. the forcemeat becoming too warm during mixing
    d. (a. and c.)
    e. (b. and c.)

16. Smear is caused by:
    a. dull grinder blade
    b. starting with too small a die
    c. poorly trimmed meats
    d. all of the above
    e. none of the above

17. In a 5:4:3 emulsified sausage, the "3" refers to:
    a. water
    b. fat
    c. meat
    d. casings

18. When tasting a forcemeat to evaluate its flavor and bind, the forcemeat should be:
    a. cold
    b. hot
    c. room temperature
    d. makes no difference

19. Bulk sausage formed into patties and wrapped in caul fat is called:
    a. *saucissons*
    b. *ècrevisses*
    c. *croquantes*
    d. *crèpinettes*

20. Which cooking method is *not* recommended for sausages?
    a. poaching
    b. boiling
    c. braising
    d. hot smoking

21. Which is *not* an approved way to check the progress of a drying sausage?
    a. taste test
    b. weight test
    c. touch test
    d. slice test

22. After encasing a sausage, you should tease holes in the casing in order to:
    a. allow steam to escape
    b. allow for expansion
    c. prevent splitting
    d. (a., b., and c.)

E. Short Essay Questions

1. Explain the importance of maintaining cold temperature when preparing and working with forcemeats.

_____

_____

_____

_____

_____

_____

2. Explain pre-seasoning of sausage meats and fat and why it is done.

_____

_____

_____

3. Explain the importance of conducting a poach test on forcemeats.

_____

_____

_____

_____

_____

4. Explain how thorough mixing of a forcemeat creates a strong bind. Include in your explanation the visual changes the meat undergoes from the time it emerges from the grinder through the completion of mixing.

_____

_____

_____

_____

5. Explain how a forcemeat emulsifies liquid during mixing. Include in your discussion the two sources of liquid in a forcemeat. Using a separate piece of paper, draw a picture of the molecular structure that sets up when this happens.

_____

_____

_____

_____

CHAPTER 13: PÂTÉS, TERRINES, AND CHARCUTERIE SPECIALTIES

This chapter extends your knowledge of forcemeats to include those made specifically for pâtés, terrines, and other pâté products. To succeed at pâté production you must therefore have mastered the information and skills taught in Chapter 12. Make sure you have correctly completed the Chapter 12 workbook questions before you begin working on Chapter 13.

The craft of pâté making demands familiarity with many French words and culinary terms. Thus, in this chapter successful completion of the "key terms" section is vital. Although in the beginning of your study of pâtés you will likely be working with recipes, understanding the procedures involved is also essential. Before you start pâté production, you should be able to number the steps in the "procedures" section without referring to the text.

Before studying this chapter, you should already
1. Have read "How to Use This Book," pages xxviii–xxxiii, and understand the professional recipe format.
2. Know basic meat and poultry cuts, and be proficient at fabricating them.
3. Be familiar with various spices, and know how to toast and grind whole spices.
4. Be proficient at clarifying stock.
5. Have read Chapter 11, "Cured and Smoked Foods," and understand the use of curing mixtures.
6. Have read Chapter 12, "Sausages," know the various types of pork fat, and be proficient at preparing standard-grind forcemeats.
7. Know how to work with gelatin if you will be preparing pâtés en croûte, or have read ahead to Chapter 16, "Aspic and Chaud-Froid," pages 632–635.

After reading this chapter, you should be able to
1. List and describe the five basic types of pâté.
2. List and describe the four elements of pâté construction.
3. Identify and safely use the proper equipment for pâté production.
4. Prepare pâté forcemeats.
5. Correctly assemble various types of pâtés.
6. Cook pâté products to the proper internal doneness and finish them appropriately according to type.
7. Prepare complementary sauces, condiments, and accompaniments for pâtés.
8. Present finished pâté products for both plated service and platter service.

A. Key Terms

Fill in each blank with the term that is defined or described.

_____ 1. Technical, one-word definition of a forcemeat baked in a pastry crust and usually served cold.

_____ 2. Specific term for a pâté baked in a crust.

_____ 3. One-word term for a pâté without a crust.

_____ 4. A poultry-based forcemeat wrapped in the skin of a fowl.

_____ 5. Controversial term referring to a forcemeat wrapped in poultry skin or a thin sheet of meat.

_____ 6. A modern pâté product, typically cylindrically shaped, wrapped in raw or cooked meat, ham, or leafy vegetable wrapper.

_____ 7. The smoothest and most refined form of pâté, made from an emulsion of puréed raw meat, eggs, and cream.

_____ 8. A pâté's main ingredient, totaling more than half of the pâté forcemeat's weight, and giving the pâté its name.

_____ 9. Additional meats added to a pâté forcemeat.

_____ 10. A pâté forcemeat partially consisting of meats that are pan-seared, chilled, and then ground.

_____ 11. The best-known pre-ground pâté spice blend.

_____ 12. A soft, smooth, starchy mixture used to bind and extend a pâté forcemeat.

_____ 13. A pâté internal garnish that has been browned, typically by pan-searing.

_____ 14. A pâté internal garnish that is mixed into the forcemeat, and appears scattered throughout the finished product.

_____ 15. A pâté internal garnish that is arranged in a specific pattern while the forcemeat is packed into its form.

_____ 16. French term for the pastry used to wrap a pâté.

_____ 17. The preferred lining fat for most terrines: solid deposit fat from a hog that has not been preserved with salt.

_____ 18. A lacy membrane that encases the stomach and intestines of hogs and other animals.

_____ 19. The poultry item that provides a galantine's skin wrapper, and much of the meat for its forcemeat.

_____ 20. Additional poultry meat needed to make the forcemeat of a galantine.

_____ 21. A large, intact section of a pâté used for presentation.

_____ 22. An ornamental skewer used to create height in a platter presentation.

_____ 23. The term used to describe a terrine that is served in the same dish in which it was baked.

B. Short-Answer Questions

1. List and describe the five types of pâtés.

a._____

(description)

_____

b._____

(description)

_____

c._____

(description)

_____

d._____

(description)

_____

e._____

 (description)
_____

2. List the four basic elements of a pâté and explain the function of each.

 a._____

 (explanation) _____

 b._____

 (explanation) _____

 c._____

 (explanation) _____

 d._____

 (explanation) _____

3. List the four fats used in pâté forcemeats.

 a._____

 b._____

 c._____

 d._____

4. List the four traditional spices used in *quatre épices*.

 a._____

 b._____

 c._____

 d._____

5. List four examples of a secondary binder.

a._____

b._____

c._____

d._____

6. List and describe the two ways to apply internal garnishes to pâtés.

a._____

(description) _____

b._____

(description) _____

7. List four items that can be used as a liner for a terrine.

a._____

b._____

c._____

d._____

8. Explain the effect of weighting terrines as they cool and chill, and list three negative results of failing to weight them.

(explanation)

_____

_____

If not weighted:

a. _____

b. _____

c. _____

C. Procedures

Correctly number the steps in the following procedures and guidelines.
Note: The directions have been condensed and some steps omitted or combined. You must think about the procedures and demonstrate your understanding; do not expect to copy from the text.

1. Procedure for making terrines:

_____ Fold the liner over the top of the forcemeat, and cover with parchment, foil, and lid.

_____ Mix the forcemeat, and refrigerate.

_____ Weight the terrine, cool, and refrigerate under weight.

_____ Poach test the forcemeat and evaluate.

_____ Make corrections to the forcemeat's seasoning and bind.

_____ Mix random internal garnishes into the forcemeat.

_____ Line the terrine mold.

_____ Fabricate and pre-season meats, fats, and internal garnishes, and refrigerate.

_____ Pack the forcemeat into the lined form, adding inlay internal garnishes.

_____ Grind the meats and fats, and refrigerate.

_____ Place the terrine in a hotel pan with hot water halfway up the sides.

_____ Bake the terrine.

_____ Prepare the terrine liner.

2. Procedure for making pâtés en croûte:

_____ Prepare the forcemeat and internal garnishes.

_____ Cut out a dough lid and dough décor, and refrigerate them.

_____ Pack the forcemeat into the form, adding inlay garnishes.

_____ Seal the pâté.

_____ Prepare the pâté pastry dough and refrigerate it.

_____ Affix the pastry lid on top of the forcemeat, create vent holes, and decorate.

_____ Bake the pâté.

_____ Release the pâté from its form.

_____ Cool the pâté to room temperature and then refrigerate for 24 hours.

_____ Refrigerate the sealed pâté for 24 hours.

_____ Roll out the dough, line a pâté en croûte form with it, and refrigerate.

_____ Refrigerate the pâté for 1 hour to rest the pastry.

3. Procedure for making galantines and ballottines:

_____ Prepare flat sheets of poultry breast meat and garnishes, and refrigerate them.

_____ Mix the forcemeat, and refrigerate.

_____ Grind all of the forcemeat ingredients, and refrigerate.

_____ Perform a poach test, evaluate, and make necessary adjustments.

_____ Refrigerate the galantine in its *cuisson* for at least 24 hours to mellow it.

_____ Cover the skin with the liner meat.

_____ Open-pan cool the galantine in its *cuisson* to room temperature.

_____ Spread the forcemeat on the liner meat.

_____ Roll the galantine into a cylinder, wrap in cheesecloth and plastic film, tie with string.

_____ Poach the galantine.

_____ Prepare the poultry skin wrapper and refrigerate it.

_____ Arrange the inlay garnish on the forcemeat-lined skin.

D. Multiple-Choice Questions

1. This cooking vessel for this pâté product is lined with pastry dough:
    a. *pâte à pâté*
    b. *pâté en terrine*
    c. *pâté en croûte*
    d. *pâté roulade*

2. The cooking vessel for this pâté product is traditionally lined with some type of fat:
    a. *pâte à pâté*
    b. *pâté en terrine*
    c. *pâté en croûte*
    d. *pâté roulade*

3. This pâté product *always* contains poultry, and is *always* wrapped in the skin of a fowl.
    a. galantine
    b. ballottine
    c. palatine
    d. (a. and b.)
    e. (a. and c.)

4. Which four pâté element is *not* necessary?
    a. forcemeat
    b. liner
    c. internal garnish
    d. sealer

5. Which is *not* a traditional function of secondary meats in pâté forcemeats?
    a. to "stretch" more expensive primary meats
    b. to contribute additional nutrients
    c. to lighten the color of the finished product
    d. to add a rich mouthfeel

6. The *fundamental* meaning of the term "gratin" is:
    a. to bake with cheese
    b. a wide, flat vessel
    c. to bake in cream sauce
    d. to brown

7. Pâté forcemeats made with North American pork or game meats should have a fat to lean meat ratio of:
   a. 35:75
   b. 40:60
   c. 50:50
   d. 60:40

8. To properly evaluate a pâté forcemeat for seasoning, bind, and mouthfeel, the cooked sample must be:
   a. hot
   b. room temperature
   c. refrigerated
   d. frozen

9. Which spice is *not* included in *quatre épices*?
   a. white pepper
   b. cinnamon
   c. ginger
   d. allspice
   e. nutmeg

10. Terrines may be lined with:
    a. pork fatback
    b. pork lard
    c. caul fat
    d. (a. and b.)
    e. (a. and c.)

11. Which terrine form should *not* be used in commercial food service?
    a. enameled cast iron
    b. stainless steel
    c. earthenware
    d. ceramic

12. Which is *not* a recommended dough for pâtés en croûte?
    a. pâte brisée
    b. biscuit-type dough
    c. yeasted bread dough
    d. puff pastry

13. The shape of a slice cut from a traditional chicken galantine is:
    a. round
    b. square
    c. triangular
    d. rectangular

14. You need to prepare country terrines as far ahead of time as possible for an important party. You can plan to store them:
    a. 1 week in the refrigerator
    b. 1 month in the refrigerator
    c. 1 month in the freezer
    d. 2 months in the freezer

15. You should *always* accompany country terrines and rustic pâtés with:
    a. green salad
    b. Dijon mustard
    c. crusty bread
    d. cornichons

E. Short Essay Questions

1. You have discovered a European pâté recipe that is 100 years old. How must you change the ingredients formula to successfully prepare this recipe today?

_____
_____
_____
_____
_____

2. Explain why a cooked pâté product should never be frozen.

_____
_____
_____

3. List the three presentation styles used for pâtés, state the type of service for which each is typically used, and draw a picture illustrating each.

a. _____

is typically used in/for _____
(drawing)

b. _____

is typically used in/for _____
(drawing)

c. _____

is typically used in/for _____
(drawing)

4. Discuss the challenges of serving or selling pâté products in today's health conscious climate. Include in your discussion ways to market pâté products.

_____
_____
_____
_____
_____
_____
_____
_____
_____
_____

CHAPTER 14: CHEESE AND OTHER DAIRY PRODUCTS

Your goal in studying this chapter is twofold: becoming familiar with and correctly serving purchased dairy products and cheeses, and becoming proficient at preparing your own fermented dairy products and fresh cheeses. Understanding the complex processes involved in producing the world's many types of cheeses is the best way to make sense of the many cheese classifications. Test your knowledge of cheese making, cheeses, and fermented dairy products by correctly answering the questions in this workbook chapter.

Before studying this chapter, you should already
1. Have read "How to Use This Book," pages xxviii–xxxiii, and understand the professional recipe format.
2. Have a sound knowledge of sanitation procedures, especially as related to protein foods.
3. Know how to calibrate and use an instant-read or probe thermometer.

After reading this chapter, you should be able to
1. Select fresh milks and creams according to their milk-fat content, and make knowledgeable decisions when substituting one for another.
2. Prepare whipped butter and composed butters.
3. Explain the process of fermentation as it applies to fermented dairy products.
4. Use commercial fermented dairy products in various cold preparations.
5. Produce fermented dairy products in-house.
6. List and explain the five steps in the cheese-making process.
7. Produce fresh cheeses in-house.
8. Correctly store and handle various types of cheese.
9. Prepare attractive, well-balanced cheese platters and cheese boards.
10. Develop a cheese menu for a restaurant or catering operation.

A. Key Terms
Fill in each blank with the term that is defined or described.

_____ 1. Foods made from milk.

_____ 2. Examples are bacteria and yeasts that create good changes in foods.

_____ 3. Dairy products that have not been changed by beneficial microorganisms.

_____ 4. A nutritious fluid produced by female mammals.

_____ 5. Milk sugar.

_____ 6. An emulsifier found in milk solids.

_____ 7. Milk consisting of 88% water, 3.5% milk fat, and 8.5% milk solids.

_____ 8. Milks blended at the dairy have a lower fat content than whole milk.

_____ 9. A fresh dairy product with milk-fat content higher than 18%.

_____ 10. The process of heating milk to a specific temperature for a specific period of time in order to destroy harmful microorganisms.

_____ 11. Milk that has not been pasteurized.

_____ 12. A method used to maintain the fat/water emulsion in dairy products.

_____ 13. A semisolid fat made from milk, and consisting of 80% milk fat, 5% milk solids, and 15% water.

_____ 14. A temperature-sensitive fat that is hard when frozen, firm when refrigerated, pliable at cool room temperature, soft at warm room temperature, and that melts when heated.

_____ 15. Butter that has had its water and milk solids contents removed; typically used for sautéing.

_____ 16. Butter that is made in small batches, by traditional methods, from raw, lightly fermented cream.

_____ 17. Butter flavored with a variety of ingredients.

_____ 18. Beneficial bacteria purposely added to a food product.

_____ 19. Thickening that occurs when the protein structure of milk and other ingredients is changed by acid or heat.

_____ 20. Term used to describe people who cannot digest milk sugars.

_____ 21. To cause the milk solids and milk fat to separate from the water content of milk.

_____ 22. A solid food, consisting mainly of milk solids and milk fat, that results from curdling.

_____ 23. The French word for "cheese."

_____ 24. The French word for "goat," frequently used to describe goat cheese.

_____ 25. An alternate term for culturing, used because it describes the primary result of bacterial action.

_____ 26. A thick, custard-like mass of milk fat and milk solids; the result of culturing.

_____ 27. A curdling agent originally derived from the stomach lining of young ruminant animals.

_____ 28. A plant-derived coloring agent used to give cheese an attractive yellow-gold color.

_____ 29. A cheese making method that involves heating, stretching and kneading curds to achieve a string-like texture; also describes cheeses made by this method.

_____ 30. The simplest form of cheese, essentially curds that have been drained and formed.

_____ 31. A series of changes that occur in a cheese due to the action of bacteria, molds, and enzymes.

_____ 32. The result of microorganism-driven changes that occur inside a cheese.

_____ 33. The result of microorganism-driven changes that occur on the exterior of a cheese.

_____ 34. Term for the edible outer rind of surface-ripened cheeses.

_____ 35. The extended storage of a fully ripened firm cheese in order to change and improve it.

_____ 36. Term often used to describe the slow ripening of firm cheeses.

_____ 37. A process that involves stacking, milling, and weighting curds to achieve a unique mouthfeel and sharp flavor in cheeses of British origin.

_____ 38. Term for holes in cheese.

_____ 39. Describes cheeses in which the culture is injected into the interior.

_____ 40. Soft surface-ripening cheeses that are moistened with brine, wine, or spirits as they ripen; most have a pungent flavor and aroma.

_____ 41. A large, double-handled cheese knife.

_____ 42. Term for the point of a cheese wedge.

_____ 43. Term for small cylindrical-shaped cheeses.

_____ 44. Commercial cheese-making cultures that are used as is and that cannot be re-used.

_____ 45. A mixture of natural cheeses and flavorings typically packed into crocks.

B. Short-Answer Questions

1. List the following fresh dairy products in order of milk-fat content, with #9 being the lowest and #1 being the highest.

_____ 2% lowfat milk

_____ heavy cream

_____ skim milk

_____ light cream

_____ half and half

_____ whole milk

_____ 1% lowfat milk

_____ butter

_____ whipping cream

2. List the five changes that occur during the fermentation of dairy products, and explain why they occur.

a. _____

occurs because: _____

b. _____

occurs because: _____

c. _____

occurs because: _____

d. _____

occurs because: _____

e. _____

occurs because: _____

3. Name the following fermented dairy products.

_____ a. A rich, thick fermented dairy product made from creams of varying milk-fat content and a culture originating in France; tangy, nutty flavor.

_____ b. A thick, fermented product made from milks of varying fat content; culture is native to the Middle East and the Caucasus.

_____ c. A fermented milk beverage containing both a bacterial culture and a yeast culture specific to the Caucasus.

_____ d. A thick, custard-like product made from light cream and a specific North American culture.

_____ e. Made from skim milk and a culture specific to North America; slightly thickened but pourable texture and a tangy flavor.

4. List the six factors that influence the characteristics of milk.

    1. _____

    2. _____

    3. _____

    4. _____

    5. _____

    6. _____

5. List and describe the five basic steps in cheese making.

step #1: _____

(description) _____

_____

_____

_____

step #2: _____

(description) _____

_____

_____

_____

step #3: _____

(description) _____

_____

_____

_____

step #4: _____

(description) _____

_____

_____

_____

step #5: _____

(description) _____

_____

_____

_____

6. Match the cheese with its type. **Note**: Each production type is used more than once.

a. fresh

b. soft surface-ripening

c. firm interior-ripened

d. washed-rind strong

e. blue

f. goat

g. hard

_____ mozzarella

_____ cheddar

_____ Roquefort

_____ Parmesan

_____ Camembert

_____ Gorgonzola

_____ Fontina

_____ ricotta

_____ Reblochon

_____ Valençay

_____ Gouda

_____ aged cheddar

_____ Havarti

_____ Brie

_____ Limburger

_____ banon

_____ Emmenthaler

_____ asiago

_____ Gruyère

_____ *fromage blanc*

C. Procedures

Correctly number the steps in the following procedures and guidelines.

Note: The directions have been condensed and some steps omitted or combined. You must think about the procedures and demonstrate your understanding; do not expect to copy from the text.

1. Procedure for making fermented dairy products:

_____ Hang the product in a cheesecloth bag to drain.

_____ Allow the milk to stand at the specified temperature for the specified amount of time.

_____ Turn off the heat and stir in the culture.

_____ Transfer the milk to a sanitized container and cover loosely with plastic film.

_____ Bring the milk or cream to the specified temperature over moderate heat.

2. Procedure for making fresh cheeses:

_____ Spoon the curds into the strainer or form, and allow them to drain.

_____ Cool the milk and stir in the culture or acidifier.

_____ Stir the rennet into the cultured milk.

_____ Hold the milk at the specified temperature until curdling is complete.

_____ Press the curds.

_____ Pasteurize the milk by holding it at 145°F (62°C).

_____ Hold the milk at the specified temperature until culturing is complete.

D. Multiple-Choice Questions

1. Which is *not* a fresh dairy product?
    a. butter
    b. buttermilk
    c. 2% milk
    d. heavy cream

2. Which is *not* a fermented dairy product?
    a. yogurt
    b. buttermilk
    c. sour cream
    d. half and half

3. Which of these products has high enough milk-fat content to whip?
    a. heavy cream
    b. whipping cream
    c. light cream
    d. (a. and b.)
    e. (a., b., and c.)

4. Clarified butter is essentially:
    a. pure milk solids
    b. pure casein
    c. milk solids and milkfat
    d. pure milkfat

5. Which is *not* an element present in milk solids?
    a. lecithin
    b. lactose
    c. casein
    d. white pigments
    e. milkfat

6. Butter melts between:
    a. 60–70°F (15°C–21°C)
    b. 70–80°F (21°C–26°C)
    c. 92–98°F (33°C–36°C)

7. Dairy fermentation is caused by:
    a. bacteria
    b. rennet
    c. yeast
    d. (a. and b.)
    e. (b. and c.)

8. Dairy coagulation is the result of acid-driven changes to:
    a. milk proteins
    b. lactose
    c. milkfat
    d. water

9. In dairy fermentation, the presence of acid is the result of:
    a. milk chemically reacting with the cooking vessel
    b. lemon juice in the recipe ingredients
    c. bacteria feeding on lactose and producing waste
    d. protein coagulation caused by rennet

10. Which does *not* affect the flavor of milk?
    a. breed of animal
    b. location of animal
    c. size of animal
    d. season of year

11. Adding bacteria to milk during the cheese-making process is called:
    a. curdling
    b. pasteurization
    c. homogenization
    d. culturing

12. Heating milk to 145°F (62°C) during the cheese-making process is called:
    a. curdling
    b. pasteurization
    c. homogenization
    d. culturing

13. Adding rennet to the milk during the cheese-making process is called:
    a. curdling
    b. pasteurization
    c. homogenization
    d. culturing

14. Which is *not* a factor in the results of ripening?
    a. type of microorganism introduced
    b. type of curdling agent used
    c. water content of the cheese
    d. how the microorganisms are introduced

15. Which is *not* a characteristic of an aged cheese?
    a. mild flavor
    b. firm texture
    c. dry mouthfeel
    d. pungent aroma

E. Short Essay Questions

1. Explain why the use of pasteurized milk is not beneficial to cheese making.

_____
_____
_____
_____
_____

2. Explain the difference between culturing and curdling.
Culturing is: _____

_____
and results in: _____
Curdling is: _____

_____
and results in: _____

3. Plan a seven-item cheese selection for a cheese tasting event. List your chosen cheeses identified by type, and justify your choices.

Cheese name	Cheese type
_____	_____
_____	_____
_____	_____
_____	_____
_____	_____
_____	_____
_____	_____

I chose these cheeses because: _____

_____
_____
_____
_____

CHAPTER 15: MOUSSELINES

It is possible to prepare successful mousselines simply by following recipes. However, understanding the scientific principles behind mousseline preparation has two important benefits. Understanding how mousselines work enables you to avoid potential problems that occur when ingredients vary or when kitchen conditions are less than ideal. Knowing the science of mousselines also helps you create your own signature mousselines by successfully substituting ingredients and changing formulas.

While some of the questions in this workbook chapter test your knowledge of facts, procedures, and ratios, most focus on understanding. Answer these questions fully and thoughtfully to prepare yourself for success in the classroom kitchen.

Before studying this chapter, you should already
1. Have read "How to Use This Book," pages xxviii–xxxiii, and understand the professional recipe format.
2. Be proficient in fabricating meats, poultry, and seafood.
3. Have read Chapter 12, "Sausages," understand the principles behind meat emulsions, and be proficient at preparing forcemeats.
4. Have read Chapter 13, "Pâtés and Terrines," and be proficient at assembling and baking forcemeats.

After studying this chapter, you should be able to
1. List the primary ingredients in mousselines and explain their functions.
2. Select proper meat, poultry, and seafood items for use in mousselines.
3. Prepare and cook mousselines.
4. Serve cold mousseline items correctly, and select appropriate sauces and garnishes for them.

A. Key Terms
Fill in each blank with the term that is defined or described.

_____ 1. A light-textured, puréed forcemeat made of raw fish, shellfish, poultry, liver, or meat.

_____ 2. Proteins found in the muscle tissue fibers of meat, poultry, and seafood; their coagulation forms a protein gel that becomes the primary structure of a mousseline.

_____ 3. The ingredient that provides the majority of the proteins that create a mousseline's structure through the process of coagulation.

_____ 4. In a mousseline, non-meat protein ingredients, typically eggs, that strengthen its structure.

_____ 5. In a mousseline, a liquid ingredient, typically cream, that loosens the protein structure and contributes the qualities of lightness and rich mouthfeel.

_____ 6. Meat protein partially responsible for the structure of a mousseline.

_____ 7. Another meat protein partially responsible for the structure of a mousseline.

_____ 8. Cooking a small sample of mousseline in order to evaluate its flavor and mouthfeel.

_____ 9. Delicate ovals of poached mousseline.

_____ 10. Term for the result of a water bath being drawn up under the foil of a covered vessel and seeping into the interior of the dish.

_____ 11. A fine-mesh drum sieve.

B. Short-Answer Questions

1. The structure of a mousseline is dependent on two successive events.

The first, occurring during mixing, is the creation of an _____

consisting of the fat in _____ and the liquids in both

_____ and _____.

The second, occurring during cooking, is _____ _____ in

two ingredients, _____ and _____.

2. List five meats that are the proper choice for mousseline.

a._____

b._____

c._____

d._____

e._____

3. Mousselines are temperature sensitive.

During mixing, the mousseline forcemeat must be _____.

The baking temperature for mousselines is _____.

4. Troubleshoot the following mousseline flaws: What went wrong?

a. grainy mouthfeel: _____

b. water in the mousseline vessel: _____

c. shrunken mousseline surrounded by liquid: _____

d. flat taste, little flavor: _____

e. rubbery texture: _____

f. too soft, not properly set: _____

C. The Mousseline Procedure

Correctly number the steps in the following procedure.
Note: The directions have been condensed and some steps omitted or combined. You must think about the procedures and demonstrate your understanding; do not expect to copy from the text.

1. Procedure for mixing and testing mousseline forcemeats:

_____ Perform a poach test, evaluate, and make necessary corrections.

_____ Trim, fabricate, and weigh the meat items.

_____ Pour cold heavy cream into the processor a thin stream.

_____ Force the mousseline through a tamis into an ice bain-marie.

_____ Proceed with cooking, or refrigerate.

_____ Place the chilled meats, egg, and seasonings in a food processor and purée them.

D. Multiple-Choice Questions

1. Mousselines may be cooked by the following methods:
    a. sautéing
    b. steaming
    c. poaching
    d. baking
    e. (a. and c.)
    f. (b. and c.)

2. When you purée a mousseline forcemeat and stream in heavy cream, you are:
    a. coagulating the meat and egg proteins
    b. creating a fat-water emulsion
    c. suspending the meat particles in milkfat
    d. breaking down the cellulose

3. When you bake a mousseline forcemeat, you are:
    a. coagulating the meat and egg proteins
    b. creating a fat-water emulsion
    c. suspending the meat particles in milkfat
    d. breaking down the cellulose

4. To make a large amount of mousseline, you can:
    a. use a floor mixer
    b. use a food processor and work in batches
    c. use a rotation chopper
    d. (a. and c.)
    e. (b. and c.)

5. Which secondary binder combination results in the tightest bind?
    a. 3 egg whites
    b. 1 egg + 2 whites
    c. 1 egg + 2 yolks
    d. 3 egg yolks

6. While poach testing and tasting your seafood mousseline forcemeat, you discover that it is too firm and has a rubbery texture. To correct this problem, you add more:
    a. egg whites
    b. scallops
    c. heavy cream
    d. egg yolks
    e. (a. and b.)
    f. (a. and c.)

7. While poach testing and tasting your seafood mousseline forcemeat, you discover that it is too soft and does not hold together. To correct this problem, you add more:
   a. egg whites
   b. scallops
   c. heavy cream
   d. egg yolks
   e. (a. and b.)
   f. (a. and c.)

8. Which mousseline main ingredient requires the highest proportion of secondary binder ingredients?
   a. salmon
   b. sea scallops
   c. red snapper
   d. shrimp

9. Following basic formula for mousseline, to one pound of fish you should use:
   a. 1/2 oz. (15 g) egg whites and 5 oz. (150 mL) heavy cream
   b. 1 1/2 oz. (45 g) egg whites to 12 oz. (36 mL) heavy cream
   c. 2 oz. (60 g) egg whites to 1 qt. (1 L) heavy cream
   d. 1 1/2 oz. (45 g) egg whites to 12 oz. (36 ml) heavy cream

10. Mousselines should bake:
   a. covered, in a water bath, at 300 degrees F (150 degrees C)
   b. covered, on a sheet tray, at 350 degrees F (175 degrees C)
   c. covered, in a water bath, at 425 degrees F (220 degrees C)
   d. uncovered, on the center rack, at 175 degrees F (80 degrees C)

E. Short Essay Questions

1. Mousseline forcemeats are versatile. Using the information in this chapter, and your imagination, name and describe three different cold dishes you could prepare using a single, large batch of seafood mousseline (plus additional ingredients).

a. _____

(description) _____

_____

_____

b. _____

(description) _____

_____

_____

c. _____

(description) _____

_____

_____

2. As a garde manger chef, how can you use your knowledge of mousseline preparation to lower your operation's food costs?

_____

_____

_____

_____

_____

_____

3. Explain the difference between a seafood mousse and a seafood mousseline.

A seafood mousse is prepared: _____

_____

_____

_____

A seafood mousseline is prepared: _____

_____

_____

_____

CHAPTER 16: ASPIC AND CHAUD-FROID

Aspic and chaud-froid work is a highly advanced facet of decorative garde manger work. Preparing the classic coating sauces requires sound knowledge of fundamentals such as stock clarification, roux thickening, and gelatin work. Readying foods to be coated necessitates sound understanding of basic cooking methods. It is to be hoped that you have acquired these skills in your introductory classes. In addition, decorating coated foods demands excellent manual skills, attention to detail, and artistic judgment.

You cannot become proficient at aspic and chaud-froid work by reading a book. The only way to master it is through hands-on practice under the supervision of a chef who is an accomplished practitioner. However, arriving in the classroom kitchen with no background information wastes valuable time. Learning about the products and studying the procedures ahead of time gives you a distinct advantage when beginning aspic and chaud-froid work. Test your comprehension by answering the questions in this workbook chapter.

Before reading this chapter, you should already
1. Have read "How to Use This Book," pages xxviii–xxxiii, and understand the professional recipe format.
2. Have read Chapter 6, "Cold Seafood," and Chapter 7, "Cold Meats," and know how to prepare these foods for cold service.
3. Be proficient at preparing and clarifying stock.
4. Be proficient at preparing velouté and demi-glace sauces.

After reading this chapter, you should be able to
1. Use granular gelatin to properly gelatinize liquids into preparations of varying consistencies.
2. Prepare aspics, chaud-froid sauces, and mayonnaise collée.
3. Set up an efficient aspic and chaud-froid workspace.
4. Prepare various foods for coating.
5. Prepare and fabricate vegetables, fruits, and herbs for surface décor.
6. Coat foods with aspic, chaud-froid, and mayonnaise collée, and decorate them with attractive designs.
7. Prepare various dishes that are bound or molded with aspic, chaud-froid, and mayonnaise collée.

A. Key Terms
Fill in each blank with the term that is defined or described.

_____ 1. A dressing for cold food that is fluid when warm and that sets up into a gel when chilled.

_____ 2. Clarified, seasoned stock with the addition of gelatin.

_____ 3. A cream velouté sauce or demi-glace sauce with the addition of aspic.

_____ 4. A coating for cold food that consists of equal parts thick mayonnaise and aspic.

_____ 5. To add commercial gelatin to a stock to strengthen its gel.

_____ 6. A nearly colorless, nearly flavorless, water-soluble substance derived from collagen.

_____ 7. An animal protein extracted from bones, cartilage, connective tissue, and hides by simmering them in water.

_____ 8. Translucent thickening created when collagen combines with water and forms a protein net.

_____ 9. A product derived by removing the water and meat flavor from liquid gelatin.

_____ 10. Term that describes the action of rehydrating dried gelatin.

_____ 11. Describes the state of a liquid that has been fortified with gelatin and then chilled; often used to describe the gel's degree of firmness.

_____ 12. Product that results when liquid gelatin is dehydrated and ground into fine granules.

_____ 13. Product that results when liquid gelatin is poured into shallow trays, dehydrated, and cut into rectangular pieces.

_____ 14. Term that describes the consistency of a gelatinized liquid thick enough to stick to a food item but not so thick that it forms lumps.

_____ 15. A translucent, gelatinized coating that adds sparkle and shine to the products it enhances.

_____ 16. Term used to describe stocks and meat-cooking juices that are strong enough in collagen to gel when chilled.

_____ 17. The technique used to remove impurities such as fat, scum, and particulate matter from stock through the process of protein coagulation.

_____ 18. To cover a food in such a way that its surface is no longer visible.

_____ 19. A type of cold sauce used to cover food.

_____ 20. Literally translates as "hot-cold;" a glossy, opaque coating sauce.

_____ 21. A type of decoration applied to the surface of a coated food.

_____ 22. Drips or tags of set coating sauce visible on a food's surface.

_____ 23. French name for a portable butane burner.

B. Short-Answer Questions

1. List three ingredients that can be used to season aspic.

a._____

b._____

c._____

2. List and describe the three categories of aspic as defined by gel strength.

a. _____

(description)_____

b. _____

(description)_____

c. _____

(description)_____

3. List and describe the three classic coating sauces.

a. _____

(description)_____

b. _____

(description)_____

c. _____

(description)_____

4. List the four steps in preparing and using a gelatinized liquid.

step #1: _____

step #2: _____

step #3: _____

step #4: _____

5. List the four types of aspic as classified by color and stock type.

a. _____

b. _____

c. _____

d. _____

6. List five guidelines for aspic and chaud-froid surface décor.

a._____

b._____

c._____

d._____

e._____

7. List six applications, other than coating food items, for aspic and chaud-froid.

a._____

b._____

c._____

d._____

e._____

f._____

C. Procedures

Correctly number the steps in the following procedures and guidelines.
Note: The directions have been condensed and some steps omitted or combined. You must think about the procedures and demonstrate your understanding; do not expect to copy from the text.

1. Procedure for coating food with chaud-froid:

_____ Melt the aspic.

_____ Ladle the aspic over the food.

_____ Melt and strain the chaud-froid.

_____ Ladle the chaud-froid over the food item.

_____ Refrigerate the food item until the chaud-froid is set.

_____ Dip the décor items into syrupy aspic and place them on the food.

_____ Trim and otherwise prepare the food to be coated; place on a rack set over a sheet tray.

_____ Stir the aspic over an ice bain-marie until it reaches syrupy consistency.

_____ Refrigerate until the aspic is set.

_____ Stir the chaud-froid over an ice bain-marie until it reaches syrupy consistency.

2. Procedure for coating forms with aspic:

_____ Press the forms down into the ice to the level of their rims.

_____ Melt the aspic.

_____ Fill a bus tub or other large container with crushed ice.

_____ Cool the aspic in an ice bain-marie to syrupy consistency.

_____ Evaluate the coating thickness and, if too thin, repeat the process.

_____ Coat the remaining forms.

_____ Pour the aspic back into its bowl.

_____ Fill one form with aspic and allow to solidify on the bottom and sides of the form.

D. Multiple-Choice Questions

1. Which is a translucent coating sauce?
   a. aspic
   b. chaud-froid
   c. mayonnaise collée
   d. (a. and b.)
   e. (a. and c.)

2. Which is an opaque coating sauce?
   a. aspic
   b. chaud-froid
   c. mayonnaise collée
   d. (a. and b.)
   e. (b. and c.)

3. Which is *not* a type of unflavored dry gelatin?
   a. leaf gelatin
   b. granular gelatin
   c. gelatin powder
   d. string gelatin
   e. sheet gelatin

4. The gelatin to liquid ratio for blooming granular gelatin is:
   a. 1:1
   b. 1:2
   c. 1:3
   d. 1:4

5. Which should *not* be used to bloom granular gelatin?
   a. table wine
   b. fortified wine
   c. clarified stock
   d. water

6. To set 2 cups of liquid to a medium-consistency gel, how much granular gelatin is needed?
   a. 1/8 oz. (3.5 g)
   b. 1/4 oz. (7 g)
   c. 1/2 oz. (14 g)
   d. 1 oz. (28 g)

7. Which ingredient *increases* gelling power?
   a. salt
   b. sugar
   c. cream
   d. lemon juice
   e. (b. and c.)

8. Which ingredient *decreases* gelling power?
   a. salt
   b. sugar
   c. cream
   d. lemon juice
   e. (b. and c.)

9. A gelatin-fortified stock will lose its gel if:
   a. boiled for 15 minutes
   b. steamtabled for 1 hour
   c. repeatedly cooled and melted
   d. (a. and b.)
   e. (a., b., and c.)

10. The clarification process typically reduces the amount of stock started with by:
    a. 10%
    b. 20%
    c. 30%
    d. 40%

11. Clarified stock for aspic can be seasoned with:
   a. Madeira
   b. fine-grind white pepper
   c. minced fresh parsley
   d. dried tarragon

E. Short Essay Questions

1. From what you have learned in this chapter, and from your own experience, explain why working with gelatin-based coating sauces requires patience.

_____

_____

_____

_____

_____

_____

_____

_____

2. On a separate piece of paper, draw a station map for an efficient aspic and chaud-froid work area, and write an equipment list for it.

(equipment list)

_____   _____

_____   _____

_____   _____

_____   _____

_____   _____

_____   _____

_____   _____

4. On a separate piece of paper, draw a template of the breast of a whole chicken to be coated with chaud-froid. Plan the décor for the chicken breast by drawing in the décor items, preferably using colored pencils. Identify the ingredient from which each type of décor item is made and, if colored pencils are not available, its color.

CHAPTER 17: CONDIMENTS, EMBELLISHMENTS, AND DÉCOR

This chapter focuses on the extras: additions that can transform an ordinary dish into something special. Knowing how to prepare the condiments and accompaniments can help you create dishes that stand out from the competition. The chapter also provides an introduction to advanced food decoration. Careful study of the procedures and guidelines enable you to try your hand at food carving, plate painting, and food décor. The basic ice carving principles and guideline presented in the chapter can lead to lifelong pursuit of this valuable skill. Demonstrate your mastery of condiments, embellishments, and décor by correctly completing the sections in this workbook chapter.

Before studying this chapter, you should already
1. Have read "How to Use This Book," pages xxviii–xxxiii, and understand the professional recipe format.
2. Be proficient at rolling out and making up pastry products.
3. Have mastered basic aspic techniques.

After reading this chapter, you should be able to
1. Prepare ketchups, mustards, pickles, relishes, chutneys, and other condiments, and use them to complement various foods.
2. Prepare hand-made crackers, chips, croûtons, and pastry cases for various garde manger applications.
3. Make aspic garnishes and décor items.
4. Become proficient at basic fruit and vegetable carving.
5. Prepare savory ices and foams.
6. Become proficient at basic plate painting.
7. Create a simple ice sculpture.

A. Key Terms
Fill in each blank with the term that is defined or described.

_____ 1. An assertively flavored food that accompanies a dish for the primary purpose of enhancing its flavor.

_____ 2. A small, decorative piece of food added to a presentation for the primary purpose of making the dish more attractive.

_____ 3. A fancy, ornate garnish.

_____ 4. A miniature composed dish used as a garnish.

_____ 5. Decoration.

_____ 6. Literally, "mounted piece," a large decorative food item.

_____ 7. A small piece of food added to a platter presentation in order to make it more attractive; edible, but typically not meant to be eaten.

_____ 8. To soak a flavorful ingredient in a hot liquid in order to release its flavors.

_____ 9. Similar to steeping, done either hot or at room temperature; typically refers to oils and vinegars.

_____ 10. General term for the liquid resulting from steeping and infusing.

_____ 11. To boil or simmer a flavorful liquid in order to evaporate away some of its water content and concentrate its flavor.

_____ 12. Alternate name for a reduction, usually one containing stock.

_____ 13. An aerated liquid.

_____ 14. An apparatus that makes foam by forcing nitrous oxide into a liquid; formerly used solely for making whipped cream, now a garde manger tool.

_____ 15. A foam created by fortifying a thin, low-fat liquid with gelatin before applying gas.

_____ 16. Highly seasoned liquids frozen in ice cube trays.

_____ 17. Semisweet syrups, vegetable juices, or fruit juices frozen in an ice cream machine.

_____ 18. The art of using sauces to create images on a plate.

_____ 19. A plate painting technique in which a thicker sauce is used to form a border that contains a thinner sauce.

_____ 20. The butter that accompanies the bread served at meals.

_____ 21. Semisoft animal fat used for sculpting or molding *pièces montées*.

_____ 22. A form of dehydration in which ice changes directly into vapor.

_____ 23. Ice produced by a special method that keeps it from clouding as it freezes.

_____ 24. Term for the condition of ice when subjected to sudden changes of temperature.

_____ 25. To condition ice for sculpting by moving it from the freezer to refrigerator temperature prior to working on it.

B. Short-Answer Questions

1. Explain the difference between a garnish and a décor item.

a. garnish: _____

_____

b. décor: _____

_____

2. Describe a *pièce montée*, and give three examples.

(description) _____

a. (example) _____

b. (example) _____

c. (example) _____

3. Match the goal with the proper technique to achieve it. **Note**: Letters a., b., and c. will be used more than once.

_____ concentrate the flavor of a brown stock

_____ prepare tarragon vinegar

_____ prepare cranberry-flavored turkey stock

_____ make a barbeque glaze thicker and more flavorful

_____ make a tea-flavored syrup for green tea sorbet

_____ prepare basil oil

a. steep

b. reduce

c. infuse

4. Describe the following embellishments.

a. cracker: _____

b. classic croûton: _____

c. savory tuile: _____

d. straw: _____

e. chip: _____

f. salad croûton: _____

5. Describe the following condiments.

a. ketchup: _____

b. prepared mustard: _____

c. pickle: _____

d. prepared relish: _____

e. cooked chutney: _____

f. jam or confiture: _____

g. flavored vinegar: _____

h. flavored oil: _____

144

6. Draw a picture of each of the following pastry shells.

a. bouchée   d. profiterole

b. barquette   e. phyllo cup

c. tartlet

7. Describe plate painting.

_____

_____

_____

_____

Describe two characteristics of sauces that can be successfully used for plate painting.

_____

_____

8. List five guidelines for successful ice sculpture.

a. _____

b. _____

c. _____

d. _____

e. _____

C. Procedures

Correctly number the steps in the following procedures and guidelines.

Note: The directions have been condensed and some steps omitted or combined. You must think about the procedures and demonstrate your understanding; do not expect to copy from the text.

1. Procedure for infusing vinegars and oils:

_____ Cover the container and allow the flavoring ingredients to steep at cool room temperature for 24 to 48 hours.

_____ Prepare the flavoring ingredients as appropriate.

_____ Heat the vinegar or oil and immediately pour it into the container.

_____ Strain the vinegar or oil through doubled cheesecloth.

_____ Place the flavoring ingredients in a sanitized container.

2. Procedure for making aspic garnishes and décor items:

_____ Chill the pan until the aspic is set.

_____ Line a flat, grease-free pan with a sheet of acetate.

_____ Cut the aspic into the desired shapes.

_____ Prepare Aspic for Slicing.

_____ Strain the aspic into the pan.

_____ Remove the aspic décor items from the acetate sheet.

146

3. Procedure for basic ice sculpting:

_____ Temper the ice block.

_____ Trace the outline of the design onto the ice.

_____ Attach the template to the ice block at least 12 hours ahead of time.

_____ Carve the ice sculpture.

_____ Transport the ice sculpture to the display area.

_____ Transport the ice block to a prepared carving area.

D. Multiple-Choice Questions

1. Which are characteristics of a décor item?
    a. meant to be eaten
    b. elaborate and time consuming
    c. simple
    d. large

2. Which is *not* a condiment?
    a. confection
    b. compote
    c. confiture
    d. chutney

3. In addition to ground mustard seeds, prepared mustard normally consists of:
    a. poultry stock
    b. wine vinegar
    c. sugar
    d. preservatives

4. In Great Britain, crackers are called:
    a. crisps
    b. flatbreads
    c. hardtack
    d. biscuits

5. When purchasing pre-made pastry dough and pastry shells, you should avoid products containing:

    a. salt

    b. hydrogenated fats

    c. butter

    d. white flour

6. The pan used to set aspic for aspic décor must be:

    a. perfectly flat

    b. grease free

    c. stainless steel

    d. (a. and b.)

    e. (a. and c.)

7. Base liquids for savory foams must be:

    a. highly seasoned

    b. hot

    c. thin

    d. (a. and b.)

    e. (a. and c.)

8. Butter décor does *not* include:

    a. molded butter

    b. pressed butter

    c. composed butter

    d. shaped butter

9. Ice sculptures may be shaped with:

    a. hand tools

    b. gas chain saw

    c. electric heat gun

    d. (a. and b.)

    e. (a., b., and c.)

10. The process of warming ice slowly at refrigerator temperature before sculpting is called:

    a. thermal shock

    b. tempering

    c. sublimation

    d. tallowing

11. An ice block can crack or break during sculpting due to:
    a. tempering
    b. stenciling
    c. bad weather
    d. thermal shock

12. Ice blocks should be stored:
    a. wrapped in plastic sheeting directly on the freezer floor
    b. unwrapped, on a plastic mat
    c. wrapped in brown paper on a piece of cardboard
    d. wrapped in plastic sheeting on a plastic mat

E. Short Essay Questions

1. Explain how a house-made condiment can add value to menu items.

_____

_____

_____

_____

Using your imagination and creativity, give an example of a specific cold dish enhanced by a specific house-made condiment.

a. sandwich: _____

    condiment: _____

b. appetizer: _____

    condiment: _____

c. main dish: _____

    condiment: _____

2. In your opinion, how does the use of inventive garnishes and décor benefit a food service operation?

_____

_____

_____

_____

What are the drawbacks?

_____

_____

_____

3. Draw a sketch of your own ice sculpture, and make a list of tools and equipment you would need to create it.

List: Sketch:

_____
_____
_____
_____
_____
_____
_____
_____
_____
_____
_____
_____

CHAPTER 18: BUFFETS AND FOOD BARS

Buffets are among the most important events in the garde manger department's calendar. A garde manger chef that is knowledgeable about buffet planning and experienced in setting up and operating buffets is an asset to any food-service operation and will likely be hired over applicants less qualified in buffet work. The knowledge, skills, and practical applications presented in this chapter give you a sound foundation in buffet work. Much of the buffet information is applicable to food bars, as well. Before you attempt to plan and execute your first professional buffet, make sure you can correctly answer the questions in this workbook chapter.

Before studying this chapter, you should already
1. Have read Chapters 1 through 17 of this text and thoroughly understand the fundamentals of garde manger work.
2. Have a sound understanding of food-service mathematics and be proficient at recipe costing.

After reading this chapter, you should be able to
1. Plan a successful garde manger buffet menu.
2. Use backwards planning to write food preparation lists for buffet work.
3. Calculate food quantities for buffets.
4. Determine the per-person food cost of a buffet menu and price the menu according to an established food cost percentage.
5. Schedule the staffing for various types of buffets.
6. Set up self-service buffets, attended buffets, and action buffets.
7. Utilize various serving pieces, structure props, and food-based and nonfood visual props to create attractive buffet displays.
8. Work as part of a team to plan, present, and break down a cold foods buffet.
9. Plan and operate a safe and successful food bar.

A. Key Terms
Fill in each blank with the term that is defined or described.

_____ 1. A long table, or line of tables, on which the food platters are arranged in a row.

_____ 2. A section of the buffet line featuring a particular type of food, such as appetizers, salads, seafood, carved meats, etc.

_____ 3. Typically offered in hotels, a permanent buffet that is always available to guests.

_____ 4. A buffet at which guests place food on their own plates.

_____ 5. Cards imprinted with the names of buffet dishes.

_____ 6. A buffet set up so that guests can access the food from both sides of the table.

_____ 7. A buffet in which one or more servers places the food on customers' plates.

_____ 8. Part of a buffet in which food is prepared to order.

_____ 9. A buffet that includes self-service, attended service, and food prepared to order.

_____ 10. Additional food stations located away from the main buffet table.

_____ 11. Decorative items placed on a buffet table to make it more attractive and to support the buffet theme.

_____ 12. A document containing the names of house-owned serving items needed for a buffet; essentially reserves these items for buffet use only.

_____ 13. A buffet at which table-and-chair seating with a place setting is provided for every guest.

_____ 14. A buffet that does not include a table place setting for every guest.

_____ 15. Foods that are pre-cut into bite-size pieces, or that are tender enough to be cut with the side of a fork.

_____ 16. A step-by-step plan for completing a number of food preparation tasks.

_____ 17. A strategy that enables planners to create a logical flow of preparation work by first focusing on the date of an event, and then working backwards to assign tasks to the appropriate days.

_____ 18. A staff member capable of performing all buffet duties.

_____ 19. A staff member responsible for monitoring the buffet line and stations, and replenishing or replacing the platters.

_____ 20. A staff member assigned to keep the buffet line(s), stations, guest tables, and room clean and orderly.

_____ 21. Frequently used term meaning "the service," the time when guests are in house.

_____ 22. The removal and storage of leftover buffet food, disassembly of the buffet line(s) and stations, and general clean-up.

_____ 23. In buffet food costing, a percentage of additional food added into your quantity calculation to prevent running out of food.

_____ 24. A self-service buffet in which prepared foods are kept on permanent display in specialized equipment.

_____ 25. A clear Plexiglas® panel suspended over or in front of a food display to protect it.

_____ 26. A report that compares the popularity of various menu items expressed as a percentage of total sales.

_____ 27. A pricing policy under which guests are able to consume as much as they wish for one set price.

B. Short-Answer Questions

1. List the advantages and disadvantages of self-service buffets.

(advantage) _____

(advantage) _____

(disadvantage) _____

(disadvantage) _____

(disadvantage) _____

2. List the advantages and disadvantages of attended buffets.

(advantage) _____

(advantage) _____

(advantage) _____

(advantage) _____

(advantage) _____

(disadvantage) _____

3. List the five phases of buffet work.

a. _____

b. _____

c. _____

d. _____

e. _____

4. List, in order, the ten tasks involved in buffet planning.

Task #1: _____

Task #2: _____

Task #3: _____

Task #4: _____

Task #5: _____

Task #6: _____

Task #7: _____

Task #8: _____

Task #9: _____

Task #10: _____

5. You must purchase main protein items for an 80-guest buffet. You are serving grilled boneless chicken breast, roast top round of beef, and poached salmon fillet, none of which will incur any significant trim waste. Calculate the amount of each item you should order. Show all your calculation work below.

boneless chicken breast: _____

top round of beef: _____

salmon fillet: _____

6. Compare and contrast buffets and food bars.

(similarities) _____

_____

_____

(differences) _____

_____

_____

_____

_____

C. Multiple-Choice Questions

1. The service of guests in a self-service buffet is speeded by:
    a. using small serving utensils
    b. using double-line configuration
    c. placing expensive foods at the end of the buffet line
    d. setting plates, forks, and napkins at the beginning of the buffet line

2. A disadvantage of attended buffets is:
    a. higher labor cost
    b. guest dissatisfaction
    c. higher food cost
    d. more waste

3. The greatest advantage of attended buffets is:
    a. enhanced reputation
    b. lower labor cost
    c. guest satisfaction
    d. portion control

4. Which does *not* need to support the theme of a buffet?
    a. server attire
    b. choice of menu items
    c. table décor
    d. food presentation style

5. Which is *not* considered a fork food?
    a. chicken salad
    b. hand-carved roast beef
    c. cold poached salmon
    d. green salad

6. The layout of buffet dishes should:
    a. display the most expensive items first.
    b. be planned so that guests are served quickly and efficiently.
    c. include desserts.
    d. face the kitchen "out" door.

7. Which takes pressure off the main buffet line?
    a. experienced bartenders
    b. satellite stations
    c. single-line configuration
    d. *piece montée*

8. Which is *not* a structural prop?
    a. tiered food stand
    b. skirting
    c. Styrofoam block
    d. cake turntable

9. Which is *not* useful for a traditional cold buffet?
    a. rechaud
    b. chafing dish
    c. carving board
    d. iced presentation tray

10. In backwards planning, the day of the event is always designated:
    a. D-Day
    b. Day #1
    c. Showtime
    d. Event Day

11. When setting up a backwards-planned event, Hour #1 should be:
    a. guest arrival
    b. bar set-up
    c. table setting
    d. rest period

12. Which break-down can begin while guests are still in house?
   a. kitchen
   b. bar
   c. buffet line
   d. coffee service station

13. The average dinner main course portion is:
   a. 3 to 4 oz. (84 to 112 g)
   b. 5 to 6 oz. (140 to 168 g)
   c. 8 to 10 oz. (224 to 280 g).
   d. 12 to 14 oz. (336 to 392 g)

14. Food bars are always:
   a. casual
   b. sanitary
   c. self-serve
   d. (a. and b.)
   e. (b. and c.)

15. The back row of a food bar (farthest from the customer) should feature:
   a. foods you need to move
   b. inexpensive items
   c. colorful items
   d. expensive items

D. Short Essay Questions

1. Recount the history of the buffet, from the Middle Ages to the present day.
Middle Ages: _____

_____

1700s: _____

_____

mid-1800s: _____

_____

late 1800s – early twentieth century: _____

_____

mid-twentieth century: _____

_____

late twentieth century – present: _____

_____

2. Describe the appearance, training, and personal characteristics of the ideal staff member you would choose to run a buffet action station.

_____

_____

_____

_____

_____

_____

_____

_____

3. Explain your ideas, preferences, and strategies for developing a buffet menu.

_____

_____

_____

_____

_____

_____

_____

_____

4. Write a seven-item menu for an attended buffet to serve 100 guests, and draw a buffet line map for it. Indicate placement of servers and guest flow.
Menu:

_____

_____

_____

_____

_____

_____

_____

Buffet line map: